CAKES
STEP-BY-STEP

Your Promise of Success

Welcome to the world of Confident Cooking,
created for you in the Test Kitchen, where
recipes are double tested by our team of
home economists to achieve a high standard
of success and delicious results every time.

C O N T E

Cherry Teacake, page 77.

Quick and Easy Carrot Cake, page 61.

Melt and Mix Chocolate Cake, page 29.

Strawberry Charlotte Russe, page 98.

N T S

Light Fruit Cake, page 91.

Sponge Fingers, page 23.

The Publisher thanks the following for their assistance in the photography for this book: Waterford Wedgwood, Corso de' Fiori, Warwick Fabrics, Limoges, Butler & Co, Mikasa Tableware, Bibelot, Noritake Tableware, Morris Home and Garden Wares, Les Olivades, Namco Aluminium Bakeware. All suppliers in Sydney, NSW.

Apple Crumble Cake, page 46.

Spiced Apple Roll, page 21.

The test kitchen where our recipes are double tested by our team of home economists to achieve a high standard of success and delicious results every time.

When we test our recipes, we rate them for ease of preparation. You will find the following cookery ratings on the recipes in this book, making them easy to use and understand.

A single Cooking with Confidence symbol indicates a recipe that is simple and generally quick to make – perfect for beginners.

Two symbols indicate the need for just a little more care and a little more time.

Three symbols indicate these are special dishes that need more investment in time, care and patience – but the results will be well worth it.

Baking Basics

Making cakes is a pleasure – a rewarding form of relaxation.
Ensure worry-free success every time you bake by
following the information set out on these introductory pages.
That way, you can have your cake and eat it, too!

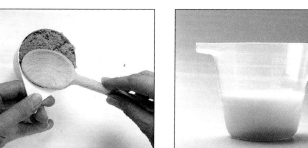

Measures and Equipment

A few essential pieces of equipment will streamline cake baking. It's well worth making the investment.

Measuring cups: For dry ingredients such as flour and sugar, it's important to have a set of four standard metric measuring cups – 1 cup, ½ cup, ⅓ cup and ¼ cup measures.

Place the cup measure on a flat surface (measuring will be inaccurate if you attempt to hold it) and spoon the dry ingredient lightly into it, levelling off with a flat bladed knife. Don't shake or tap the cup.

Soft brown sugar is measured as a dry ingredient. Pack it down tightly in the specified measuring cup, to the point where it is level with the top. Use only dry measures for dry ingredients.

To measure liquid items such as milk and juice, use a standard metric measuring cup of heatproof plastic or glass with a pouring lip. The lines of measurement run down the cup's side. Place the cup on a board, add liquid to the required measure and check at eye level with the measurement marks.

Measuring spoons: Those used for cooking are different from flatware for serving and eating. They are essential for the accurate measuring of small amounts of dry and liquid ingredient. You need 1 tablespoon, 1 teaspooon, ½ teaspoon and ¼ teaspoon measures.

Kitchen scales: Useful for weighing butter. Conveniently, some blocks of butter have weight markings on the side of the wrapper; simply use a small, sharp knife to cut through the butter at the mark you require.

Scales are a help for measuring large quantities of dried and glacé fruits, nuts and chocolate. For those who prefer to measure by weight, not by volume, see the chart on page 112 for conversion of metric cup measures.

Metric or imperial? Do not attempt to combine metric and imperial measures. Use one system of measurement only, and stick with it.

Egg sizes: In all the recipes in this book, we have used eggs each with an average weight of 60 g.

Ovens: An accurate oven is possibly the most important piece of equipment for successful cake baking. Because ovens can lose their calibration, they should be checked every six months to ensure that correct temperatures and accurate readings are reached.

All ovens vary and not all oven thermometers are to be trusted. Be prepared to make slight adjustments to the temperatures and cooking times until you know your own oven well.

Always preheat the oven before you begin preparing your cake mixture.

For the best results when baking, position an oven rack in the lower third of the oven; this enables the top of the cake tin to be in approximately the middle of the oven. Centre the cake tin on the oven rack. If you are baking two cakes at the same time, stagger the tins so they are not placed directly beneath one another. If both are placed on the same rack, keep them away from the sides and back of the oven. They may need turning during the last third of the the cooking time to ensure an even result.

Electric beaters: An electric stand mixer is a vital piece of equipment; it

Place the dry ingredient in a measuring cup. Level it with a flat-bladed knife.

Pack soft brown sugar into measuring cup; press firmly with back of spoon.

To measure liquid, place jug on a flat surface. Measure liquid at eye level.

Cake Tin Shapes and Sizes

1   **Ring Tin** 20 cm
2   **Deep Round Tin** 17/20/23 cm
3   **Shallow Round Tin** 17/20/23 cm
4   **Round Springform Tin** 20 cm
5   **Baba (Fluted) Tin** 20 cm
6   **Deep Fluted Ring Tin** 23 cm
7   **Loaf Tin** 21 x 14 x 7 cm
    Loaf Tin 23 x 13 x 7 cm
    Loaf Tin 25 x 15 x 5.5 cm
8   **Shallow Oblong Tin** 30 x 20 x 3 cm
    28 x 18 x 3 cm
9   **Long Bar Tin** 26 x 8 x 4.5 cm
10 **Shallow Patty Tin** 12 cup
11 **Deep Square Tin** 15/20/23 cm
12 **Shallow Swiss Roll Tin** 30 x 25 x 2 cm
13 **Oven Tray** 32 x 28 cm

enables you to cream butter and sugar mixtures effortlessly to the correct consistency. It beats egg whites and egg white mixtures quickly and easily.

Adequate results can be obtained using a hand-held mixer or by mixing by hand if quantities are not too great. However, if you choose the latter, the mixing time increases considerably and care must be taken to achieve the correct consistency.

Food processors: These are ideal for blending ingredients together, but are unsuitable for creaming mixtures.

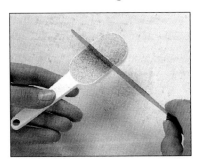

Place the dry ingredient in a measuring spoon. Level it with a flat-bladed knife.

Cake tins: Using the correct size of cake tin plays an important part in the success of the finished cake. There are many shapes and sizes of tin from which to choose. Aluminium ones give consistently good results. Avoid using shiny or very dark tins and glass bakeware. Listed are the tin sizes we used. Different manufacturers may produce slightly different sizes.

Changing tin sizes: If you wish to substitute one shape of tin for another, measure the volume of the batter and pour the same amount of water into the tin you intend to use. As long as the water does not come any higher than two thirds of the way up the tin, you can use it.

Useful extras: Two wire cake racks for cooling cakes; several wire sifters for flour and cocoa powder; a range of wooden and metal spoons; small to large glass mixing bowls; a small hand grater for rind; rubber and plastic spatulas; a long, serrated knife to level and slice cakes horizontally, and a flat-bladed or palette knife for smoothing on the icings and fillings.

Preparing Cake Tins

The way to prepare a cake tin varies according to the type of cake you are baking. Here are the general guidelines.

Butter cakes and chocolate cakes: They require tins that are greased and lined. You need to line the

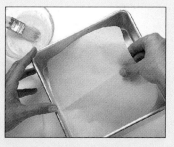 

To line square tins: Place tin base on a square of greaseproof paper; trace around it. Cut base out as marked. Cut a strip of greaseproof paper the same length as the circumference of the tin and about 1 cm deeper than the height.

Grease the base and sides of the tin with melted butter or oil, applying it with a pastry brush. Place the square of greaseproof paper on the base. Place the long strip of greaseproof around the sides of the tin, pressing it into the sides; grease base and sides of paper lining.

To line round tins: Place tin base on a square of greaseproof paper, trace around it. Cut base out as marked. Cut a strip of greaseproof paper the same length as the circumference of the tin and about 3 cm deeper than the height.

Fold down a cuff about 2 cm deep on one edge of the strip. Cut folded cuff diagonally at 2 cm intervals. Grease tin with melted butter or oil, applying it with a pastry brush.

Place strip in tin with folded side on base; press paper into base and side of the tin. Place the round of greasproof paper on base, grease base and side of paper lining.

 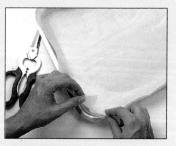

To line Swiss roll tins: Place tin base on a square of greaseproof paper; trace around it. Measure depth of tin, then measure paper from the marked line, and cut all around to 2 cm larger than the depth.

Crease paper along marked lines, cut paper to each corner. Grease tin with melted butter, applying it with a pastry brush. Press paper down into base and sides of tin; grease paper lining.

base and side/sides of the tins and grease the paper for these cakes. Fluted tins and baba tins are greased; if using anodised baba tins or if the cake mixture is very rich, you may need to lightly flour the baba tin, too.
Sponges: Tins must be greased, and their base lined and floured for easy removal of the cake.

Traditional fruit cakes and cakes rich with dried or glacé fruits: Tins need their base and side/sides lined with greaseproof paper; it is generally not necessary to grease the paper. A double thickness of brown paper is wrapped around the outside of the tin and secured with a paper clip before baking; this protects and insulates the cake during the long, slow baking time.

Greasing tins: Use melted, unsalted butter or oil. Apply evenly, smoothly and not too thickly, using a pastry brush. Vegetable baking sprays can be used to grease tins; apply in a well ventilated area away from heat sources.

Lining with paper: Greaseproof paper is the preferred paper for lining tins. Non-stick baking paper is also available and good results are achieved with this coated paper; it is not necessary to grease it.

Dusting: Let the greased tin or the greased paper dry off a little before dusting the tin with flour. Use plain flour, turning the tin to evenly coat the base and sides. Shake off the excess before spooning in the cake mixture. Some recipes call for the tin to dusted with desiccated coconut, finely ground breadcrumbs or nuts. Follow the same procedure as you would with flour.

Ingredients

Each ingredient used in cake baking has a specfic role.
Flour: This forms the structure of the cake. We have used plain flour and self-raising in our recipes. Plain flour (also known as all-purpose flour), has no raising agent. Self-raising flour is plain flour with baking powder added, that acts as the raising agent. To use plain flour in place of self-raising, add 2 standard metric teaspoons to each ¾ standard metric cup of plain flour. Sift flour and baking powder together three times before using.
Eggs: These are also essential to the structure of the cake. They bind the

other ingredients together, and also add flavour and colour. We have used eggs each with an average weight of 60 g. For baking, eggs should be at room temperature. Take them out of the fridge an hour before required. Eggs separate far more easily when cold; separate white from yolk while cold; bring to room temperature before use.

Butter: Butter supplies flavour, texture and aroma. We used unsalted butter in all our recipes because it gives cakes a fuller, richer and sweeter flavour. Butter should be at room temperature (about 22°C) for it to cream correctly. If colder, it will not cream or aerate well. If it is too soft and oily, it will not aerate at all.

Margarine: This produces an adequate result; avoid low-fat margarine because it contains too much water.

Oil: In carrot and zucchini cakes, oil gives very moist results. Use a good quality vegetable oil; avoid olive oil or peanut oil; their flavours are too pronounced.

Sugar: It adds sweetness, colour, softness and fine grain to cakes. Fine-textured caster sugar is commonly used in baking. Granulated, all-purpose sugar is too difficult to cream and will only produce a coarse-textured cake. Icing sugar is too fine for general cake making. Soft brown sugar produces moist, flavoursome results in rich fruit cakes. Use soft dark brown sugar for a more intense flavour, if preferred.

Milk: The most commonly used liquid in cake baking. Others are yoghurt, buttermilk, sour cream and fruit juice.

Flavourings and essences: These should be of good quality. We used imitation vanilla essence in nearly all our recipes; it is widely available and inexpensive. Pure essences produce a delicious aroma and flavour. Their flavour is more intense – a little goes a long way.

Other flavourings such as finely grated orange or lemon rind, ground

---

Steps to Successful Cakes

☐ Read the recipe entirely beforehand. Assemble all the ingredients and equipment before proceeding.

☐ Preheat oven to correct temperature, prepare baking tins.

☐ Don't allow room temperature ingredients such as butter and eggs to get too warm.

☐ Measure ingredients accurately; do not judge quantities by eye but use standard metric measuring cups and spoons.

☐ Presift dry ingredients.

☐ Ensure correct creaming of butter and sugar mixtures; add eggs or egg yolks gradually.

☐ Don't overbeat egg whites.

☐ Take care with folding in procedures.

☐ Spoon or pour cake mixture into prepared cake tin, spread evenly into corners and smooth surface.

☐ Check oven temperature; avoid opening oven door until at least two thirds of the way through baking.

☐ Times given for cakes are approximate; the cooking time can vary according to the accuracy of the oven temperature and where the cake is placed.

☐ Stand cake in tin for specifed time before turning onto wire rack to cool.

---

spices, honey, treacle, cocoa or coffee powder and chocolate offer infinite variety to your baking. When grating orange or lemon rind, grate only the coloured surface of the skin, not the white, bitter pith.

Techniques

Sometimes a cake is described simply by its flavourings; for example, as a chocolate or coffee cake. Other times, cakes can be described by the nature of their presentation – teacakes or celebration cakes, for example.

Cakes are also classified by the method used to make them. In general, they'll fall into one of four categories: creaming; whisking (beating of whole eggs and/or egg whites); rubbing and quick mixing.

It is important to understand the differences between methods and to follow the correct procedures for each.

Creaming method: This is the most

---

frequently used method in cake baking. It is used for light to rich butter cakes, teacakes, light fruit cakes, chocolate cakes and more. The proportion of butter to sugar varies from recipe to recipe.

Best results are obtained by beating butter (which is at room temperature) and sugar in a small glass mixing bowl with electric beaters until the mixture is light and creamy.

The mixture will almost double in volume and should have no trace of the sugar granules. Scrape the sides of the bowl with a spatula several times during the creaming process to make sure the sugar and butter are well incorporated. This intial creaming process can take up to seven or eight minutes. Whole eggs or egg yolks are then added. Be sure to beat these lightly before adding them to the butter mixture; add the beaten eggs gradually, beating thoroughly after each addition.

Essences, grated rind and other flavourings are added at this stage. The butter mixture is then transferred to a large mixing bowl. Use a large metal spoon to gently fold in the sifted dry ingredients and liquid alternately. Stir until just combined and the mixture is almost smooth.

Take care with this final stage, mixing the ingredients together lightly yet evenly; over-enthusiastic beating can undo previous good work and produce a heavy, coarse-textured cake.

For creaming method, beat butter and sugar until light and creamy.

Whole eggs can be beaten with sugar over simmering water (Génoise-style).

Beat egg whites with electric beaters until stiff peaks form.

Gradually add the beaten egg yolks, continuing to use electric beaters.

Whisking method: This is generally used for sponges and light and airy Swiss rolls. Eggs are the chief ingredient, used whole or separated. Use the freshest eggs and have them at room temperature. Whole egg sponges are made by beating whole eggs in a small mixing bowl with electric beaters for 5 minutes or until thick and pale.

Sugar is added gradually, about a tablespoon at a time. Beat constantly until the sugar is dissolved and the mixture is pale yellow and glossy. The sifted dry ingredients are then quickly and lightly folded in.

Eggs can also be beaten whole with the sugar in a glass bowl over simmering water (Génoise style) until the mixture is very pale yellow and thick; a whisk or hand-held electric beaters can be used. The mixture is then removed from the heat and beaten with electric beaters until it has nearly doubled in volume. The sifted dry ingredients are then folded in.

Some recipes call for the eggs to be separated and beaten separately. Take care when separating eggs because just one small particle of egg yolk can ruin their beating quality. Separate one at a time into a small glass bowl; then transfer to the bowl for beating.

Beating the egg whites: Beating egg whites to the correct consistency is a vital stage in cake making. Use a glass bowl; make sure it is clean and dry. Use electric beaters to beat the egg whites until firm peaks form – the whites should hold a firm peak or curl when you lift the beaters out. Beating constantly, the sugar is then added gradually; beat until completely dissolved. The mixture should be very glossy and very thick; when you lift the beaters, the mixture should hold straight peaks.

The lightly beaten egg yolks are then added and the mixture is transferred to a large, glass mixing bowl. Use a metal spoon to fold in the sifted dry ingredients quickly and lightly.

The folding technique: This is also critical to success. It is the lightest way to combine two mixtures. Using a large metal spoon, fold in the dry ingredients, running the spoon along the underside of the bowl and up in one sweeping action – literally taking them under and over the egg mixture. Cut down through the centre of the bowl on the next fold, rotating the bowl as you fold. Repeat these actions until all of the ingredients are combined. Work quickly and lightly to ensure even distribution of ingredients and to avoid overmixing.

Rubbing method: Use for quick teacakes and economical fruit loaves.

The butter is chopped into small pieces and rubbed through the sifted dry ingredients until the mixture is a fine, crumbly texture. Use only your fingertips, lifting the flour from the bowl as you rub to evenly distribute the butter.

Liquid ingredients are combined and stirred into the flour mixture with a flat-bladed knife until the mixture comes together. Generally, cakes made by this method are best eaten the day they are made.

Quick mix method: This fast and simple method is gaining popularity. Use for cakes such as carrot and zucchini or easy chocolate cakes.

Vegetable oil or butter is used; the butter is melted with flavourings such as brown sugar or chocolate and then poured over the sifted dry ingredients. Make a well in the centre of the dry ingredients beforehand. Stir mixture with a wooden spoon or whisk until ingredients are evenly combined. The beaten eggs are then stirred in; care must be taken not to overmix.

Decorating Your Cake

Before you can ice or fill your cake, you will need to prepare it. Handle your cake with care at this stage.

Slicing Cakes

Always work with completely cooled cakes when decorating, unless the recipe states otherwise. If the cake is even slightly warm, it will be difficult to handle and there is every possibility that it will crack or break when sliced.

Some cakes dome slightly when baked and may need trimming before

Fold in flour with metal spoon; run it along bowl base in one sweeping action.

Quick mix method: Melted butter and sugar are poured on dry ingredients.

Testing if a cake is cooked: A cake is cooked when it begins to shrink from the sides of the tin and is lightly golden on top. If pressed with a finger, it should spring back into shape at once. The exception would be a very rich cake such as a fruit one which may retain a slight impression and yet still be cooked.

As a final check, insert a fine skewer in the centre; it should come out clean, without any moisture.

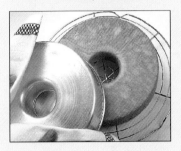

Cooling the cake: A cake is quite fragile when removed from the oven. It is best to leave it in its tin for the specifed time before turning it onto a wire rack to cool. Leave the cake on the wire rack until completely cold.

If a cake seems to be stuck to the tin, gently run a flat-bladed knife around the sides to release it. Cakes lined with paper are easiest to release; as you turn out the cake, use the paper to gently ease its passage. Remove the paper lining immediately. Wire cake racks can be sprayed with vegetable baking spray occasionally to prevent the warm cake sticking to them.

Storage: As a general guide, you can store most cakes for up to three days in an airtight container. Fillings and icings make cakes more perishable.

Fruit cakes can be stored in the refrigerator for up to two months, covered with several layers of plastic wrap. See each of our recipes for specific storage guidelines for each cake.

Cakes can be successfully frozen. Best results are obtained when they are frozen uniced and unfilled. Open-freeze cakes to preserve shape. To do this, place on a tray in the freezer without covering. When frozen, wrap in plastic wrap and aluminium foil, excluding as much air as possible. Place in a rigid container for added protection. Label and date the cake. Store for up to three months or to the specified time. To defrost, loosen wrapping and leave at room temperature until thawed.

Brush loose crumbs off the cake with a pastry brush for a smooth finish.

Using a flat-bladed knife, spread filling to within 5 mm of the cake edge.

Scoop nuts into the side of your hand and gently press them onto side of cake.

icing to give a better appearance. Use a long, sharp, serrated knife to slice off the dome. Cut only enough cake to give an even surface. Cut with a gentle sawing motion, using your other hand to steady the cake while you slice. Turn the cake over onto the serving plate, base side up, before icing.

Many cakes are cut in half or in one or more layers horizontally before they are filled. To make the job easy, mark the midpoint round the side of the cake with toothpicks. Use a long, sharp, serrated knife for slicing the cake; use a gentle sawing action. Repeat marking and cutting procedure for each layer.

Icing and Filling Cakes

To achieve a good finish when icing, turn the cake over so the base side is up. Use a pastry brush to brush off any loose crumbs. Spread icing over the cake using a flat-bladed knife. The result will be a smooth iced surface.

To assemble layered cakes, slice horizontally as described. Place a dab of icing or filling on a serving plate. Place the first cake layer on top (the icing will stop it moving), centring it on the plate. Brush with jam or liquid, then spread evenly with the specified amount of filling mixture. Using a flat-bladed knife or metal spatula, spread the filling to within about 5 mm of the edge of the cake.

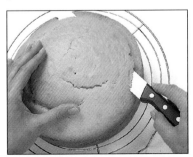

Slice off dome. Cut with gentle, sawing motion. Use other hand to steady cake.

Mark midpoint around cake with toothpicks; slice with sharp, serrated knife.

Using a vegetable peeler, shave curls of chocolate from flat side of block.

Piping Bags

Here is quick and easy way to make a small, paper piping bag. This is an ideal 'tool' to use when working with fine icing and when icing a cake with melted chocolate.

Cut a 25 cm square of strong greaseproof paper and fold it in half diagonally to form a triangle. Working with the long side at the bottom, roll a corner to the centre and tape in place. Wrap the other corner around to the back and tape it in place. Use scissors to snip off the tip of the bag to suit the size of decorating you will be doing. You can also drop a small nozzle into the bag for icing.

Using a knife or metal spatula, half-fill the bag with melted chocolate or icing. Fold in the top, then roll the top down to the level of the icing to seal the bag. With your writing hand, grip the bag at the top with the full end resting in your palm. Use pressure from the palm of your hand to push the icing through the hole. Practice will show how to vary the pressure and achieve a good flow of icing.

Pour melted chocolate onto a marble board; let set. Shave off chocolate.

Melting Chocolate

Some of the decorating ideas in this book require using melted chocolate. Care must be taken when melting chocolate in order to achieve good results.

Chop the chocolate into even-sized pieces and place in a glass bowl. Place bowl over a pan of simmering water; stir gently until chocolate has melted. Do not allow a drop of water to fall on the chocolate or it will immediately stiffen dramatically and be unworkable for decoration purposes. Cool chocolate slightly before use.

Decorating Ideas

Chocolate Decorations, Shavings: Decorate the cake with chocolate shavings, simply by using a vegetable peeler to shave off curls from the flat side of a block of chocolate. Use long, even strokes. Work over greaseproof paper or a plate. For best results, the chocolate should be warmed, but only sufficiently to enable you to work it; it must not be melting. Leave chocolate in a warm spot for 10 to 15 minutes before shaving. Spoon or shake the shavings onto the iced cake.

Another version of curls is made by pouring 100 g melted chocolate onto a marble or Laminex board in a 4 cm wide strip. Smooth the surface, allow

Place the second layer on top and spread with the filling mixture, in the same way as described above. Place the final layer, base side up, on the top. Spread a thin layer of cream or of frosting around the sides and top of the cake to seal in any crumbs and to fill any gaps. Dip the knife or spatula into hot water as you spread to make it a little easier to work. Wipe the knife with a clean cloth before you continue.

Spread a final layer of cream or frosting evenly around the sides and

then the top of the cake, blending at the edges. Use even strokes.

The edges of the cake can be decorated very effectively with toasted nuts. This is easier than it sounds. Simply press the nuts into the side of the cake using your hand. Scoop them up and push them gently into the cream or frosting, continuing around the cake until it is evenly covered. To finish, use a pastry brush to sweep away any loose nuts that have fallen on the serving plate.

Place strips of greaseproof paper in a pattern. Dust with sifted icing sugar.

Feather cake by drawing the point of a skewer from centre circle to outer edge.

Mark semi-set chocolate into wedges. Refrigerate. Peel away foil.

Mark semi-set chocolate into squares. Refrigerate. Peel away foil.

chocolate to set. Shave off strips with a vegetable peeler, using long strokes.

Sifted icing sugar: Cut strips of greaseproof paper about 1 cm wide, place in a pattern on top of the cake. Dust with sifted icing sugar. Carefully lift paper off, leaving a clear pattern. Use pretty paper doileys to achieve the same look.

Feathering: Ice the cake with dark icing and use light icing or melted chocolate to create a striking marbled effect. Place the melted chocolate or light icing in a paper piping bag and pipe concentric circles onto the icing. Draw the point on a knife or skewer from the the centre circle to the outside edge. Clean skewer and repeat, working around cake in wedges to produce a feathering effect.

Wedges: Cover the base of a 20 cm round tin with foil. Spread about 150 g melted chocolate evenly over it and refrigerate until semi-set. Using a sharp, flat-bladed knife, carefully mark the chocolate into 12 even wedges. Return to refrigerator until chocolate is completely set. Peel away foil.

Squares: These are an easy and impressive way to decorate the sides of a cake. Cover the base of a 32 x 28 cm oven tray with foil. Spread 200 g

melted chocolate evenly over it, swirl a fork lightly through the chocolate to create a wavy effect. Make sure you don't push it to the base. Refrigerate until semi-set. Using a sharp, flat-bladed knife and a ruler, mark chocolate into 6 cm squares. Return tray to refrigerator until chocolate is completely set. Peel away foil. Carefully press chocolate squares around the edges of the iced cake.

Lattice circles and silhouettes: Mark a sheet of baking paper with small circles, using a 3 cm cutter as a guide. Alternatively, mark squares, rectangles or triangles with a pencil. Melt about 150 g chocolate and place in a paper piping bag.

Applying a light pressure, pipe an outline of chocolate around the shape and fill it in with squiggly lines. Other shapes can also be most effective; try stars or flowers. Refrigerate until set. Use a flat-bladed knife to remove the decorations carefully from the baking paper, and place them on cake.

Cut-outs: The kids can make these! Cover the base of a shallow, 30 x 20 cm oblong tin with foil. Spread 250 g melted chocolate evenly over the base. Refrigerate until semi-set. Use small, sharp cutters to mark different shapes.

Use rounds and fluted rounds or other fancy shapes. Use to decorate the sides or the top of the iced cake.

Chocolate curls: These take a little time, practice and patience to master. Spread 250 g melted chocolate onto a marble or Laminex board to a depth of 1 cm, smoothing the surface lightly. Allow to cool until almost set. Use a sharp, flat-bladed knife; hold it horizontally. Applying constant pressure to the blade with both hands, pull the knife towards you. Varying the pressure on the blade will determine how thick or thin the curls will be.

Shapes: Boxes of very thin squares of chocolate are produced by several confectionery companies and are ideal, ready-made decorations.

Nuts and sprinkles: Sprinkle the top of a simple iced cake with finely chopped, toasted nuts, with coconut or with chocolate or coloured sprinkles. Decorate the outer edge of the iced cake with whole nuts or glacé cherries.

Marzipan fruits: When time is at a premium and you need a quick and easy, ready-made decoration, you can purchase a range of marzipan fruits from confectioners and also some good cake shops. These are most attractive, colourful and professional-looking.

Lattice shapes: Mark various shapes on greaseproof; pipe outlines of chocolate.

Chocolate cut-outs: Press a variety of sharp cutters into semi-set chocolate.

Chocolate curls: Hold knife horizontally. Apply constant pressure to blade.

SPONGE CAKES

CLASSIC SPONGE

Preparation time: 30 minutes
Cooking time: 20 minutes
Makes one 20 cm round layer cake

1 cup self-raising flour
4 eggs, separated
2/3 cup caster sugar
2/3 cup cream
1 teaspoon imitation vanilla
    essence
1/2 cup strawberry jam
icing sugar, for decoration

➤ PREHEAT OVEN to moderate 180°C. Brush two shallow, 20 cm round sandwich tins with melted butter or oil. Line bases with paper. Dust tins lightly with flour, shake off excess.

1 Sift the flour three times onto greaseproof paper.
Place egg whites in small, clean, dry mixing bowl. Using electric beaters, beat until firm peaks form. Add sugar gradually, beating constantly until it has dissolved and mixture is glossy and thick.

2 Add the beaten egg yolks, beat for a further 20 seconds. Transfer mixture to large mixing bowl. Using a metal spoon, fold in flour quickly and lightly.

3 Spread the mixture evenly into prepared tins. Bake for 20 minutes or until sponges are lightly golden and shrink from sides of tins. Leave the sponges in tins for 5 minutes before turning onto wire rack to cool.
Using electric beaters, beat cream and essence in small bowl until stiff peaks form. Spread jam on both sponges. Spread cream on one sponge layer using a flat-bladed knife. Top with other layer. Dust with sifted icing sugar just before serving.

COOK'S FILE

Storage time: Unfilled sponge can be frozen for 1 month. Place each layer in a freezer bag, seal, label and date. Thaw sponges at room temperature; this will take about 20 minutes. Filled sponge is best eaten immediately.
Variation: Omit jam in the filling and fill cake with cream only. Decorate top with fresh berries and cream swirls.
This sponge mixture can also be baked successfully in a deep, 23 cm round cake tin. Increase the baking time to 40 minutes.
Cut cake horizontally into three layers and fill with the jam and cream, as previously described. You will need to increase the jam to 3/4 cup and the cream to 1 cup.

CITRUS GÉNOISE SPONGE

Preparation time: 40 minutes
Cooking time: 20 minutes
Makes one 20 cm round layer cake

1 cup self-raising flour
4 eggs, lightly beaten
½ cup caster sugar
60 g unsalted butter, melted
   and cooled
2 teaspoons finely grated
   orange rind
1 teaspoon finely grated lemon
   rind

Lemon Curd Filling
6 teaspoons cornflour
⅓ cup caster sugar
¾ cup milk
⅓ cup lemon juice
2 eggs, lightly beaten

➤ PREHEAT OVEN to moderate 180°C. Brush two shallow, 20 cm round sandwich tins with melted butter or oil. Line bases with paper; grease the paper. Dust the tins lightly with flour, shake off excess.

1 Sift the flour three times onto greaseproof paper.
Combine eggs and sugar in medium heatproof mixing bowl. Place bowl over pan of simmering water. Beat until mixture is thick and pale yellow. Remove from heat, continue to beat until mixture has cooled slightly and increased in volume.

2 Add flour, melted butter, lemon and orange rind. Using metal spoon, fold quickly and lightly until ingredients are just combined.

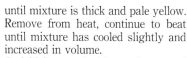

Spread mixture evenly into prepared tins. Bake for 20 minutes or until the sponges are lightly golden and shrink from sides of tins. Leave sponges in tins for 5 minutes before turning onto wire rack to cool.

3 To make Lemon Curd Filling: Combine cornflour, sugar, milk, lemon juice and eggs in small pan, mix well. Stir over low heat until mixture boils and thickens, cook for 1 minute longer. Remove from heat. Transfer to a small bowl, cover with plastic wrap and allow to cool before using.

4 Cut each cake in half horizontally. Place a cake layer on a serving plate. Spread the cake evenly with the filling. Continue layering with remaining cake and filling, ending with a cake layer on top. Dust the top with sifted icing sugar, if desired.

COOK'S FILE

Storage time: Unfilled sponge can be frozen for 1 month. Place each layer in a freezer bag, seal, label and date. Thaw sponges at room temperature; this will take about 20 minutes. Filled sponge is best eaten immediately.
Variation: Use lemon or orange rind only in cake, if preferred. Orange juice can be used in place of lemon in filling.

VICTORIA SPONGE

Preparation time: 20 minutes
Cooking time: 20 minutes
Makes one 20 cm round layer cake

1 cup self-raising flour
4 eggs, lightly beaten
¾ cup sugar
60 g unsalted butter, melted
    and cooled
¼ cup warm milk
½ cup raspberry jam
icing sugar, for decoration

► PREHEAT OVEN to moderate 180°C. Brush two shallow, 20 cm round sandwich tins with melted butter or oil. Line bases with paper; grease the paper. Dust the tins lightly with flour, shake off excess.

1 Sift the flour three times onto greaseproof paper.
Using electric beaters, beat eggs in small mixing bowl for 5 minutes or until thick and pale.

2 Add sugar gradually, 1 tablespoon at a time, beating constantly until it has dissolved and the mixture is pale yellow and glossy. Transfer mixture to a large mixing bowl.
Using a metal spoon, fold in butter, milk and flour quickly and lightly.

3 Spread mixture evenly into the prepared tins. Bake for 20 minutes or until sponges are lightly golden and shrink from sides of tins. Leave the sponges in tins for 5 minutes before turning onto wire rack to cool.
Spread jam on both sponge layers, place together. Dust with sifted icing sugar just before serving.

COOK'S FILE

Storage time: Unfilled sponge can be frozen for 1 month. Place each layer in a freezer bag, seal, label and date. Thaw sponges at room temperature; this will take about 20 minutes. Filled sponge is best eaten immediately.
Hint: Spread the jam on both of the cake layers to stop the two halves slipping apart on cutting.

CORNFLOUR SPONGE

Preparation time: 35 minutes
Cooking time: 15 minutes
Makes one 20 cm round layer cake

½ cup cornflour
2 tablespoons self-raising flour
3 eggs, lightly beaten
½ cup caster sugar
⅔ cup cream

Passionfruit Icing
1¼ cups icing sugar
1 teaspoon unsalted butter
¼ cup passionfruit pulp

➤ PREHEAT OVEN to moderate 180°C.
Brush two shallow, 20 cm round sandwich tins with melted butter or oil. Line bases with paper; grease paper. Dust tins lightly with flour, shake off excess.

1 Sift flours three times onto greaseproof paper.
Using electric beaters, beat eggs in small mixing bowl for 5 minutes or until thick and pale.
Add sugar gradually, beating constantly until dissolved and mixture is pale yellow and glossy. Transfer mixture to large mixing bowl.

2 Using a metal spoon, fold in flours quickly and lightly.
Spoon mixture evenly into prepared tins. Bake for 15 minutes or until the sponges are golden and shrink from the sides of the tins. Leave sponges in tins for 5 minutes before turning onto wire rack to cool.

3 Beat cream in medium bowl until stiff peaks form.
Using a flat-bladed knife, spread the cream evenly on one of the sponge layers. Place the other sponge on top.
To make Passionfruit Icing: Combine the sifted icing sugar, butter and sufficient passionfruit pulp in a small bowl to make a stiff paste. Stand bowl in pan of simmering water, stirring until icing is smooth and glossy; remove from heat. Spread over cake using a flat-bladed knife. Allow icing to set before serving cake.

COOK'S FILE

Storage time: Unfilled sponge can be frozen for 1 month. Place each layer in a freezer bag, seal, label and date. Thaw sponges at room temperature; this will take about 20 minutes. Filled sponge is best eaten immediately.
Hint: If any excess icing runs down the side of the cake, leave to set before removing. Simply cut away from the edge; the icing will not have stuck to the side of the cake.

CLASSIC SWISS ROLL

Preparation time: 25 minutes
Cooking time: 10 to 12 minutes
Makes one Swiss roll

¾ cup self-raising flour
3 eggs, lightly beaten
½ cup caster sugar
¼ cup caster sugar, extra
½ cup strawberry jam

➤ PREHEAT OVEN to moderately hot 210°C.
1 Brush a shallow, 30 x 25 x 2 cm Swiss roll tin with melted butter or oil. Line base and two sides with paper; grease paper. Sift flour three times onto greaseproof paper.

Using electric beaters, beat eggs in small mixing bowl for 5 minutes or until thick and pale.
2 Add sugar gradually, beating constantly until dissolved and mixture is pale and glossy. Transfer mixture to large mixing bowl.
Using a metal spoon, fold in flour quickly and lightly.
3 Spread mixture evenly into prepared tin; smooth surface. Bake for 10 to 12 minutes or until lightly golden and springy to the touch.
Turn cake out onto a dry, clean tea-towel covered with greaseproof paper that has been sprinkled with the extra sugar; leave for 1 minute. Using the tea-towel as a guide, carefully roll cake up with the paper; leave for 5 minutes or until cool.

4 Unroll cake, discard paper. Spread with jam; re-roll. Trim ends with knife; decorate as desired.

COOK'S FILE

Storage time: Filled roll is best eaten immediately.
Hint: Jam is best beaten with a spatula for 30 seconds before it is applied to the cake. This will soften the jam and make it easier to spread. Any type of jam can be used.

LAYERED CHOCOLATE SPONGE

Preparation time: 40 minutes
Cooking time: 20 minutes
Makes one 20 cm round layer cake

¾ cup self-raising flour
2 tablespoons cocoa powder
4 eggs, lightly beaten
¾ cup caster sugar

Vienna Cream
125 g unsalted butter
1¼ cups icing sugar
2 tablespoons cocoa powder
2 tablespoons milk

Glacé Icing
1¼ cups icing sugar
1 teaspoon instant coffee
    powder
1 teaspoon unsalted butter,
    melted
1-2 tablespoons water
10 walnut halves

➤ PREHEAT OVEN to moderate 180°C. Brush two shallow, 20 cm round sandwich tins with melted butter or oil. Line bases with paper, grease paper. Dust tins lightly with flour, shake off excess.

1 Sift flour and cocoa three times onto greaseproof paper.

Using electric beaters, beat the eggs in a small mixing bowl for 5 minutes or until thick and pale. Add the sugar gradually, beating constantly until it has dissolved and the mixture is pale yellow and glossy. Transfer mixture to large mixing bowl.

2 Using a metal spoon, fold in sifted ingredients quickly and lightly.

Spoon mixture evenly into prepared tins. Bake for 20 minutes or until the sponges are lightly golden and shrink from sides of tins. Leave the sponges in tins for 5 minutes before turning onto wire rack to cool.

3 To make Vienna Cream: Using electric beaters, beat the butter in a small bowl until light and fluffy. Add sifted icing sugar and cocoa, beating for 8 to 10 minutes or until mixture is smooth and fluffy. Add milk and continue beating for 3 minutes.

4 Spread one sponge with half the Vienna Cream. Place remaining cream in a piping bag and pipe rosettes of cream around the edge of the sponge. Place other sponge on top.

5 To make Glacé Icing: Combine sifted icing sugar and coffee powder with melted butter and sufficient water to form a firm paste. Stand bowl in pan of simmering water, stirring until icing is smooth and glossy; remove from heat.

6 Spread the icing over cake using a flat-bladed knife. Decorate with the walnut halves. Allow the icing to set before serving.

COOK'S FILE

Storage time: Unfilled sponge can be frozen for 1 month. Place each layer in a freezer bag, seal, label and date. Thaw sponges at room temperature; this will take about 20 minutes. Filled sponge is best eaten immediately.

Hint: Overheating the icing will make it dull, flat and grainy. Work quickly when applying icing, dipping the knife into hot water occasionally to give a smooth, shiny appearance; do not reheat icing.

Some packets of flour carry the label 'ready sifted'. Despite that, all flour should be sifted before use to rid it of any lumps and to incorporate air. The heat of the oven causes the air trapped in the cake mixture to rise. Self-raising flour contains baking powder, which is a raising agent.

1

2

3

4

5

6

SPONGE WITH MOCK CREAM FILLING

Preparation time: 30 minutes
Cooking time: 15 minutes
Makes one 20 cm round layer cake

¾ cup self-raising flour
3 eggs, lightly beaten
½ cup caster sugar
icing sugar, for decoration

Mock Cream Filling
125 g unsalted butter
½ cup caster sugar
1 teaspoon imitation vanilla
  essence

➤ PREHEAT OVEN to moderate 180°C. Brush two shallow, 20 cm round sandwich tins with melted butter or oil. Line bases with paper; grease paper. Dust the tins with flour, shake off excess.

1 Sift the flour three times onto greaseproof paper. Using electric beaters, beat eggs in a small bowl for 5 minutes or until thick and pale. Add the sugar gradually, beating constantly until dissolved and mixture is pale yellow and glossy. Transfer the mixture to a large mixing bowl.

2 Using a metal spoon, fold in flour quickly and lightly. Spread mixture evenly into the prepared tins. Bake for 15 minutes or until sponges are lightly golden and shrink from sides of tins. Leave sponges in tins 5 minutes before turning onto wire rack to cool.

3 To make Mock Cream Filling: Using electric beaters, beat butter and sugar in small mixing bowl until light and creamy. Remove bowl from electric mixer. Cover the mixture with cold water, swirl water around and pour off. Beat with electric beaters for a further 2 minutes.

Repeat this whole process six times or until cream is white and fluffy and sugar is dissolved. Stir in essence. Sandwich cakes with filling. Dust with sifted icing sugar just before serving.

COOK'S FILE

Storage time: Unfilled sponge can be frozen for 1 month. Place each layer in a freezer bag, seal, label and date. Thaw sponges at room temperature; this will take about 20 minutes. Filled sponge is best eaten immediately.
Variation: Stir 90 g grated chocolate through the filling mixture.

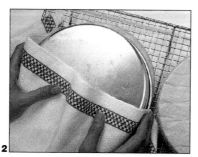

SPICED APPLE ROLL

Preparation time: 40 minutes
Cooking time: 12 minutes
Makes one Swiss roll

¾ cup self-raising flour
1 teaspoon five spice powder
3 eggs, lightly beaten
½ cup caster sugar
icing sugar, for decoration

Apple Filling
2 large green apples, peeled
    and cored
1 tablespoon caster sugar
1 teaspoon lemon juice
⅔ cup cream

➤ PREHEAT OVEN to moderately hot 210°C.
Brush a shallow, 30 x 25 x 2 cm Swiss roll tin with melted butter or oil. Line base and two sides with paper; grease the paper.
Sift flour and spice three times onto greaseproof paper.
Using electric beaters, beat eggs in small mixing bowl for 5 minutes or until thick and pale.
1 Add the sugar gradually, beating constantly until dissolved and mixture is pale yellow and glossy. Transfer mixture to large mixing bowl.
Using a metal spoon, fold in the dry ingredients quickly and lightly.
2 Spread the mixture evenly into the prepared tin; smooth the surface. Bake for 10 to 12 minutes or until lightly golden and springy to the touch.
Turn cake out onto a clean, dry tea-towel covered with greaseproof paper; leave for 1 minute.
Using tea-towel as a guide, carefully roll up the cake with the paper; leave for 5 minutes or until cool. Unroll and discard the paper.

3 To make Apple Filling: Place apples in small pan, add ¼ cup water and cook on low heat until fruit is tender. Discard any remaining liquid. Use a fork to break up apples, stir in sugar and lemon juice to taste. Cool. Beat cream in small bowl until stiff peaks form. Refrigerate until required. Spread roll with cooled apples and whipped cream; re-roll. Trim ends of roll with serrated knife. Dust with icing sugar just before serving.

COOK'S FILE

Storage time: Filled roll is best eaten immediately.
Hint: This Swiss roll is excellent served as a dessert.

1

2

3

HAZELNUT CHOCOLATE ROLL

Preparation time: 35 minutes
Cooking time: 12 minutes
Makes one Swiss roll

½ cup self-raising flour
3 eggs, lightly beaten
⅓ cup caster sugar
100 g chocolate, finely
  chopped
½ cup ground hazelnut meal
1 tablespoon strong black coffee
1¼ cups cream
1 tablespoon strong black
  coffee, extra
⅓ cup icing sugar
2 tablespoons cocoa powder

➤ PREHEAT OVEN to moderately hot 210°C.
Brush shallow, 30 x 25 x 2 cm Swiss roll tin with melted butter or oil. Line the base and two sides with paper; grease the paper.
1 Sift the flour three times onto greaseproof paper.
Using electric beaters, beat eggs in small mixing bowl for 5 minutes or until thick and pale.
Add sugar gradually, beating constantly until dissolved and mixture is pale yellow and glossy. Transfer to a large mixing bowl.
2 Using a large metal spoon, fold in chocolate, hazelnut meal, coffee liquid and flour quickly and lightly. Spread mixture evenly into the prepared tin; smooth surface. Bake 12 minutes or until golden and springy to the touch. Beat cream and extra coffee liquid in small bowl until stiff peaks form. Refrigerate until required.
3 Turn cake onto a clean, dry tea-towel covered with greaseproof paper which has been dusted evenly with

sifted icing sugar and cocoa; leave for 1 minute. Using tea-towel as a guide, carefully roll up cake with paper; leave cake for 5 minutes or until cool.
Unroll cake, discard paper. Spread with coffee cream filling; re-roll. Trim the ends of roll with a serrated knife.

COOK'S FILE

Storage time: Filled roll is best eaten immediately.
Hint: Make strong black coffee using instant coffee powder or granules or by brewing espresso coffee.

1

2

3

SPONGE FINGERS

Preparation time: 20 minutes
Cooking time: 6 minutes
Makes 24 sponge fingers

⅓ cup self-raising flour
2 tablespoons cornflour
2 eggs, separated
⅓ cup caster sugar
20 g unsalted butter, melted
⅔ cup cream
½ teaspoon imitation vanilla
    essence
icing sugar, for decoration

➤ PREHEAT OVEN to moderate 180°C. Brush two 32 x 28 cm biscuit trays with melted butter or oil, line bases with paper; grease paper. Dust tins lightly with flour, shake off the excess. Mark lines in the flour 7 cm apart on each tray.

1 Sift the flours three times onto greaseproof paper. Place egg whites in a small, clean, dry mixing bowl. Using electric beaters, beat until firm peaks form. Add sugar gradually, beating constantly until dissolved and mixture is glossy and thick.

Add beaten egg yolks, beat a further 20 seconds. Transfer mixture to large mixing bowl. Using a metal spoon fold in flours gradually and lightly. Add butter, fold through.

2 Place mixture in large piping bag fitted with a round nozzle.

Pipe fingers between the 7 cm lines, leaving 5 cm between each one.

Bake for 6 minutes or until lightly golden. Leave sponge fingers on tins for 5 minutes before placing them on wire rack to cool.

3 Beat cream and essence in small bowl until stiff peaks form.

Sandwich two sponge fingers together with a spoonful of whipped cream. Repeat with the remaining fingers and cream. Dust with sifted icing sugar just before serving.

COOK'S FILE

Storage time: Filled fingers are best eaten immediately.

Variation: Spoon mixture into fingers or rounds, instead of using a piping bag. Fold ¼ cup finely chopped strawberries through the whipped cream, if desired.

1

2

3

CHOCOLATE CAKES

MOIST CHOCOLATE CAKE WITH CREAMY CHOCOLATE SAUCE

Preparation time: 30 minutes
Cooking time: 35 minutes
Makes one 23 cm ring cake

1¾ cups self-raising flour
1 teaspoon bicarbonate of soda
½ cup cocoa powder
1 tablespoon instant coffee powder
¾ cup caster sugar
¼ cup demerara sugar
2 eggs, lightly beaten
1 teaspoon imitation vanilla essence
1 cup buttermilk
½ cup milk
60 g unsalted butter, melted

Creamy Chocolate Sauce
100 g dark chocolate, coarsely chopped
⅓ cup cream

➤ PREHEAT OVEN to moderate 180°C.
1 Brush a deep, 23 cm fluted ring tin with melted butter or oil. Sift the flour, soda, cocoa and coffee into a large mixing bowl. Add the sugars.
2 Pour combined eggs, liquids and melted butter onto the dry ingredients; using electric beaters, beat the mixture on a low speed for 3 minutes until it is just moistened.
3 Beat the mixture on high speed for 5 minutes or until free of lumps and increased in volume.
Pour mixture evenly into prepared tin; smooth surface. Bake 35 minutes or until skewer comes out clean when inserted in centre of cake. Leave cake in tin 10 minutes before turning onto wire rack to cool.
To make Creamy Chocolate Sauce: Combine chocolate and cream in small pan. Stir over low heat until chocolate melts. Remove from heat. Cool to room temperature. Pour sauce over cake. Serve at once with fresh fruit.

COOK'S FILE

Storage time: 3 days in an airtight container or up to 2 months in the freezer without sauce.
Hint: Store chocolate, wrapped, in a cool place, but not in the refrigerator; if it is too cold, it will acquire a dusty white 'bloom' and be unsuitable for decoration purposes.

BEST EVER CHOCOLATE CAKE

Preparation time: 25 minutes
Cooking time: 45 minutes
Makes one 20 cm square cake

125 g unsalted butter
½ cup caster sugar
⅓ cup icing sugar
2 eggs, lightly beaten
1 teaspoon imitation vanilla
　essence
¼ cup blackberry jam
1¼ cups self-raising flour
½ cup cocoa powder
1 teaspoon bicarbonate of soda
1 cup milk

Rich Chocolate Butter Cream
50 g dark chocolate, finely
　chopped
25 g unsalted butter
¼ cup icing sugar
2 teaspoons cream

➤ PREHEAT OVEN to moderate 180°C. Brush a deep, 20 cm square cake tin with melted butter or oil, line the base and sides with paper; grease the paper.

1 Using electric beaters, beat butter and sugar and sifted icing sugar in small mixing bowl until light and creamy. Add eggs gradually, beating thoroughly after each addition. Add essence and jam; beat until combined.

2 Transfer mixture to large mixing bowl. Using a metal spoon, fold in sifted flour, cocoa and soda alternately with milk. Stir until just combined and the mixture is almost smooth.

Pour mixture into prepared tin; smooth surface. Bake 45 minutes or until skewer comes out clean when inserted in centre. Leave cake 15 minutes before turning onto wire rack to cool.

3 To make the Rich Chocolate Butter Cream: Combine the chocolate, butter, sifted icing sugar and cream in a small pan. Stir over low heat until the mixture is smooth and glossy. Remove from the heat. Spread Butter Cream over top of cake using a flat-bladed knife.

COOK'S FILE

Storage time: 1 week in an airtight container or up to 3 months in the freezer uniced.

Hint: The surface of this cake may be slightly wrinkled after cooking; this is easily concealed by the Butter Cream.

CHOC-RUM AND RAISIN CAKE

Preparation time: 40 minutes
Cooking time: 1 hour
Makes one 20 cm round cake

½ cup raisins, chopped in half
2 tablespoons overproof rum
185 g unsalted butter
¾ cup caster sugar
2 eggs, lightly beaten
2 cups self-raising flour
⅓ cup cocoa powder
¾ cup milk

Choc-Rum Icing
125 g unsalted butter
⅔ cup icing sugar
2-3 tablespoons overproof rum
¼ cup grated dark chocolate

➤ SOAK RAISINS in rum overnight. Preheat oven to moderate 180˚C. Brush a deep, 20 cm round cake tin with melted butter or oil, line base and side with paper; grease paper.

1 Using electric beaters, beat butter and sugar in small mixing bowl until light and creamy. Add eggs gradually, beating thoroughly after each addition. Transfer mixture to a large mixing bowl. Using a metal spoon, fold in rum and raisins.

2 Fold in the sifted flour and cocoa alternately with milk. Stir until just combined and mixture is almost smooth.

3 Pour mixture into prepared tin; smooth surface. Bake 1 hour or until skewer comes out clean when inserted in centre of cake. Leave cake in the tin 15 minutes before turning onto wire rack to cool.

To make Choc-Rum Icing: Using electric beaters, beat butter and sifted icing sugar in small mixing bowl until light and creamy. Add rum and chocolate; beat until smooth and fluffy.

4 Spread two-thirds of the icing over top and sides of cake using a flat-bladed knife. Pipe edging around cake rim using remainder of icing. Decorate with purchased chocolates or chocolate decoration of your choice (see page 11).

COOK'S FILE

Storage time: 3 days in an airtight container or up to 2 months in the freezer uniced.

MILK CHOCOLATE CHIP CAKE

Preparation time: 25 minutes
Cooking time: 35 minutes
Makes one 20 cm ring cake

90 g unsalted butter
1/3 cup caster sugar
2 eggs, lightly beaten
1/2 teaspoon imitation vanilla
    essence
60 g milk chocolate, coarsely
    chopped
1/2 cup/90 g milk Choc Bits
1 1/4 cups self-raising flour
extra Choc Bits, for decoration

Milk Chocolate Icing
100 g milk chocolate, coarsely
    chopped
1/4 cup cream
30 g unsalted butter
2 teaspoons icing sugar

➤ PREHEAT OVEN to moderate 180°C. Brush a deep, 20 cm ring tin with melted butter or oil. Line base with paper; grease paper.

1 Coat base and side evenly with flour; shake off excess.
Using electric beaters, beat butter and sugar in small mixing bowl until light and creamy. Add the eggs gradually, beating thoroughly after each addition. Add essence; beat until combined.

2 Place chocolate in a glass bowl. Stir over barely simmering water until melted; remove from heat. Transfer butter mixture to large mixing bowl; add chocolate and Choc Bits.

3 Using a metal spoon, fold in sifted flour. Stir until just combined and the mixture is almost smooth.
Spoon mixture evenly into prepared tin; smooth surface. Bake 35 minutes or until skewer comes out clean when inserted in centre of cake. Leave cake in tin 10 minutes before turning onto wire rack to cool.

4 To make Milk Chocolate Icing: Combine chocolate, cream, butter and sifted icing sugar in a small pan. Stir over low heat until chocolate and butter have melted and mixture is smooth; remove from heat. Cool. Pour icing over cake. Top with extra Choc Bits.

COOK'S FILE

Storage time: 3 days in an airtight container or up to 2 months in the freezer uniced.

MELT AND MIX CHOCOLATE CAKE

Preparation time: 20 minutes
Cooking time: 1 hour 45 minutes
Makes one 20 cm round cake

1⅓ cups self-raising flour
⅓ cup plain flour
⅓ cup cocoa powder
1 tablespoon instant coffee
   powder
¾ cup caster sugar
¼ cup soft brown sugar
200 g unsalted butter
1 tablespoon golden syrup
½ cup hot water

100 g dark chocolate, coarsely
   chopped
2 eggs, lightly beaten
2 tablespoons cocoa powder
1 tablespoon icing sugar

➤ PREHEAT OVEN to moderately slow 160°C. Brush a deep, 20 cm round cake tin with melted butter or oil, line base and side with paper; grease paper.

1 Sift the flours, cocoa and coffee into a large mixing bowl. Make a well in the centre.

2 Combine sugars, butter, syrup, water and chocolate in a large pan. Stir over a low heat until the butter and chocolate are melted and the sugars dissolved; remove from heat.

3 Add butter mixture to the dry ingredients. Using a whisk, stir until just combined; add the eggs, mix well; do not overbeat.

Pour mixture into prepared tin. Bake for 1 hour 45 minutes or until skewer comes out clean when inserted in centre of cake. Leave cake in tin 1 hour before turning onto wire rack to cool. Dust cake with combined sifted cocoa and icing sugar.

COOK'S FILE

Storage time: 1 week in an airtight container or for up to 3 months stored in the freezer.

Hint: Store all types of sugar in airtight containers away from the light.

DEVIL'S FOOD CAKE

Preparation time: 30 minutes
Cooking time: 40 to 50 minutes
Makes one 20 cm round cake

1⅓ cups plain flour
⅔ cup cocoa powder
1 teaspoon bicarbonate of soda
1 cup caster sugar
2 eggs, lightly beaten
1 cup buttermilk
1 teaspoon imitation vanilla
   essence
125 g unsalted butter, softened
½ cup cream, whipped
60 g white chocolate, coarsely
   chopped

Feathered Icing
60 g unsalted butter
60 g dark chocolate, melted

▶ PREHEAT OVEN to moderate 180°C. Brush a deep, 20 cm round tin with melted butter or oil, line base and side with paper; grease paper.
Sift flour, cocoa and soda into large mixing bowl. Add sugar.
1 Pour the combined eggs, buttermilk, essence and butter onto dry ingredients; using electric beaters, beat on low speed for 3 minutes or until just moistened.
2 Beat the mixture on high speed for 5 minutes or until mixture is free of lumps and increased in volume. Pour mixture into prepared tin; smooth the surface. Bake 40 to 50 minutes or until skewer comes out clean when inserted in centre of cake. Leave cake in tin for 15 minutes before turning onto wire rack to cool.

3 To make the Feathered Icing: Combine butter and chocolate in a small pan; stir over a low heat until melted; remove from heat. Cool. Cut the dome off the cake to level the surface. Cut cake in half horizontally.
Spread whipped cream over half of cake from which dome was sliced. Sandwich with the other layer. Spread icing over top using flat-bladed knife. Place white chocolate in glass bowl. Stir over barely simmering water until melted; remove from heat. Cool slightly.
4 Spoon melted chocolate into a small paper icing bag, seal open end. Snip tip off the piping bag; pipe 8 to 10 small to large circles around the top of the cake. Drag a skewer from the centre circle to the outside of the cake. Clean the skewer and repeat this process, working around the cake in wedges. This is called feathering (see page 11).

COOK'S FILE

Storage time: 3 days unfilled in an airtight container or up to 3 months in the freezer unfilled and uniced. The filled cake is best assembled and eaten the same day.

CHOCOLATE PEANUT FUDGE CAKE

Preparation time: 40 minutes
Cooking time: 1 hour
Makes one 20 cm round cake

1¼ cups self-raising flour
¼ cup cocoa powder
200 g unsalted butter
100 g dark chocolate, coarsely
    chopped
¼ cup smooth peanut butter
¾ cup cream
¾ cup caster sugar
2 eggs, lightly beaten
cocoa powder, for decoration
packaged chocolate-dipped
    peanuts, for decoration

Dark Chocolate Icing
150 g dark chocolate, coarsely
    chopped
90 g unsalted butter
½ cup condensed milk

➤ PREHEAT OVEN to moderate 180°C. Brush a deep, 20 cm round tin with melted butter or oil, line base and side with paper; grease paper.

1 Sift flour and cocoa in a large mixing bowl. Make a well in the centre.
Combine butter, chocolate, peanut butter, cream and sugar in a medium pan. Stir over low heat until butter and chocolate have melted and sugar has dissolved; remove from heat.

2 Add the butter mixture to the dry ingredients. Using a whisk, stir until just combined; add eggs, mix well; do not overbeat.
Pour mixture into prepared tin. Bake for 1 hour or until skewer comes out clean when inserted in centre of cake.

3 Leave cake in tin 30 minutes before turning onto wire rack to cool.

To make Dark Chocolate Icing: Combine chocolate, butter and condensed milk in small pan. Stir over low heat until chocolate and butter melt and mixture is smooth; remove from heat. Cool until thick and spreadable.

4 Cut the cake in half horizontally. Spread half the chocolate mixture over base half of cake. Sandwich with top layer of cake.
Spread rest of icing over top of cake. Sprinkle with extra cocoa powder; decorate with chocolate-dipped peanuts.

COOK'S FILE

Storage time: 3 days in an airtight container or up to 2 months in the freezer uniced.

WHITE CHOCOLATE AND YOGHURT CAKE

Preparation time: 30 minutes
Cooking time: 40 minutes
Makes one 20 cm round cake

125 g unsalted butter
½ cup caster sugar
2 eggs, lightly beaten
1 teaspoon imitation vanilla
  essence
100 g white chocolate, coarsely
  chopped
½ cup plain or vanilla yoghurt
1½ cups self-raising flour

White Chocolate Topping
125 g cream cheese, softened
60 g white chocolate, melted
2 tablespoons plain yoghurt

▶ PREHEAT OVEN to moderate 180°C. Brush a deep, 20 cm round cake tin with melted butter or oil, line base and side with paper; grease paper.

1 Using electric beaters, beat butter and sugar in small mixing bowl until light and creamy. Add eggs gradually, beating thoroughly after each addition. Add essence; beat until combined.

2 Place chocolate in glass bowl. Stir over barely simmering water until melted; remove from heat.
Transfer butter mixture to large mixing bowl; add chocolate and yoghurt. Using a metal spoon, fold in sifted flour. Stir until just combined and the mixture is almost smooth.

3 Pour mixture into prepared tin; smooth surface.
Bake 40 minutes or until skewer comes out clean when inserted in centre of cake. Stand cake in tin 15 minutes before turning onto wire rack to cool.

To make the White Chocolate Topping: Using electric beaters, beat cream cheese in small mixing bowl until light and creamy. Add chocolate and yoghurt, beating 5 minutes or until mixture is smooth and fluffy. Spread icing completely over cake using a flat-bladed knife. Decorate cake with white chocolate curls (refer to page 11).

COOK'S FILE

Storage time: 3 days in an airtight container or up to 1 month in the freezer uniced.

Variation: To make a more moist, heavier cake, use ⅔ cup yoghurt. This cake can also be made with a flavoured yoghurt. Substitute vanilla yoghurt for the plain in the White Chocolate Topping.

1

2

3

CHOCOLATE SPICE CAKE

Preparation time: 40 minutes
Cooking time: 45 minutes
Makes one 20 cm round cake

100 g unsalted butter
⅔ cup caster sugar
2 eggs, lightly beaten
1 tablespoon golden syrup
1½ cups self-raising flour
¼ cup cocoa powder
½ teaspoon bicarbonate
   of soda
¼ teaspoon ground cloves
¼ teaspoon ground allspice
⅔ cup milk

Spicy Syrup
½ cup caster sugar
⅔ cup water
¼ teaspoon ground cloves
¼ teaspoon ground allspice

➤ PREHEAT OVEN to moderate 180°C. Brush a deep, 20 cm round cake tin with melted butter or oil, line base and side with paper; grease paper.
1 Using electric beaters, beat butter and sugar in small mixing bowl until light and creamy. Add eggs gradually, beating thoroughly after each addition. Add syrup; beat until combined.
2 Transfer the mixture to a large mixing bowl. Using a metal spoon, fold in the sifted flour, cocoa, soda and spices alternately with milk.
Stir until just combined and mixture is almost smooth. Pour mixture into prepared tin; smooth surface. Bake for 45 minutes or until skewer comes out clean when inserted in centre of cake. Leave cake in tin to cool.
3 To make Spicy Syrup: Combine sugar, water and spices in small pan. Stir constantly over low heat until mixture boils and sugar has dissolved.

Reduce heat, simmer without stirring, uncovered, until mixture has thickened and reduced by half. Remove from heat; leave until bubbles subside.
Pour the hot Spicy Syrup mixture over the cake while it is still in the tin. When all the syrup has been absorbed, turn cake out of tin.

COOK'S FILE

Storage time: 3 days in an airtight container or up to 2 months in the freezer without syrup.
Hint: Keep ground spices in airtight jars away from direct sunlight or their flavour will quickly deteriorate.

1

2

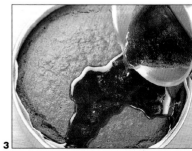
3

CHERRY CHOCOLATE RING

Preparation time: 10 minutes
Cooking time: 45 minutes
Makes one 23 cm ring cake

250 g unsalted butter
1 cup caster sugar
3 eggs, lightly beaten
1 cup/200 g halved glacé cherries
1/3 cup Choc Bits
2 cups plain flour
1/2 teaspoon bicarbonate of soda
125 g dark chocolate, coarsely chopped, optional
2 teaspoons oil, optional
whipped cream and glacé cherries, for decoration

➤ PREHEAT OVEN to moderate 180°C. Brush a deep, 23 cm fluted ring tin with melted butter or oil. Coat base and side evenly with flour; shake off the excess.

1 Using electric beaters, beat butter and sugar in a small mixing bowl until creamy and white. Add the eggs gradually, beating thoroughly after each addition.

2 Transfer mixture to large mixing bowl; add cherries and Choc Bits. Using a metal spoon, fold in sifted flour and soda. Stir until just combined and mixture is almost smooth. Spoon mixture evenly into prepared tin; smooth the surface. Bake cake for 45 minutes or until skewer comes out clean when inserted in centre.

3 Leave cake in tin 5 minutes before turning out onto wire rack to cool.

Place chocolate and oil in a small heatproof bowl. Stand the bowl over a pan of simmering water, stir until the chocolate has melted and mixture is smooth. Cool slightly.

Spread cake evenly with the melted chocolate mixture using a flat-bladed knife; alternatively, pour the mixture over. Refrigerate the cake, uncovered, for 10 minutes or until the chocolate is firm. Decorate with whipped cream and glacé cherries.

The chocolate topping is optional. This cake can also be covered with whipped cream and decorated with glacé cherries.

COOK'S FILE

Storage time: 3 days in an airtight container or up to 2 months in the freezer uniced.

ESPRESSO CHOCOLATE CAKE WITH LIQUEUR SAUCE

Preparation time: 45 minutes
Cooking time: 30 minutes
Makes one 20 cm baba cake

¼ cup finely ground espresso coffee
¾ cup boiling water
150 g unsalted butter
¾ cup soft dark brown sugar
2 eggs, lightly beaten
⅓ cup ground almonds
1½ cups self-raising flour
¼ cup cocoa powder

Chocolate Liqueur Sauce
¾ cup caster sugar
¾ cup water
¼ cup chocolate liqueur

➤ COMBINE COFFEE and water in a small heatproof bowl. Allow to stand 10 minutes. Strain, reserving ½ cup of the liquid.

1 Preheat oven to moderate 180°C. Brush a deep, 20 cm baba tin with melted butter or oil.
Using electric beaters, beat butter and sugar in small mixing bowl until light and creamy. Add eggs gradually, beating thoroughly after each addition.

2 Transfer mixture to large mixing bowl; add almonds. Using a metal spoon, fold in sifted flour and cocoa alternately with strained coffee. Stir until just combined and the mixture is almost smooth.

3 Spoon mixture into prepared tin; smooth surface. Bake 30 minutes or until skewer comes out clean when inserted in centre of cake. Leave cake in tin 15 minutes before turning onto wire rack.

4 To make Chocolate Liqueur Sauce: Combine the sugar, water and liqueur in a small pan.
Stir constantly over low heat until mixture boils and sugar has dissolved. Reduce heat, simmer without stirring, uncovered, until mixture begins to thicken and liquid is reduced by half. Remove from heat, leave the sauce for 2 minutes for the bubbles to subside. Pour sauce into heatproof serving jug. Serve sauce warm with warm cake and pouring cream.

COOK'S FILE

Storage time: This cake is best eaten the day it is made.
Variation: Substitute a coffee liqueur for the chocolate one, if preferred.
Hint: The darker the sugar, the more likely it is to become hard; this is because the film of molasses covering it contains moisture which hardens if it dries. A slice of apple placed in the jar will help to prevent this happening.

CHOCOLATE ORANGE CAKE

Preparation time: 35 minutes
Cooking time: 45 minutes
Makes one 20 cm square cake

180 g unsalted butter
½ cup caster sugar
2 eggs, lightly beaten
1 teaspoon finely grated orange
   rind
¼ cup demerara sugar
½ cup orange juice
2 cups self-raising flour
⅓ cup cocoa powder
orange segments and strips of
   rind, for decoration

Orange Topping
250 g cream cheese, softened
¼ cup icing sugar
1 teaspoon finely grated orange
   rind
⅓ cup orange juice

➤ PREHEAT OVEN to moderate 180°C. Brush a deep, 20 cm square cake tin with melted butter or oil, line base and sides with paper; grease paper.
1 Using electric beaters, beat butter and sugar in small mixing bowl until light and creamy. Add eggs gradually, beating thoroughly after each addition. Add rind; beat until combined.

2 Combine demerara sugar and orange juice in a small pan. Stir over a low heat until sugar has dissolved. Remove from heat.

3 Transfer butter mixture to large mixing bowl. Using a metal spoon, fold in the sifted flour and cocoa alternately with the juice mixture. Stir until just combined and mixture is almost smooth.

Pour mixture into prepared tin; smooth surface. Bake 45 minutes or until skewer comes out clean when inserted in centre of cake. Leave cake in tin 10 minutes before turning onto wire rack to cool.

4 To make Orange Topping: Beat cream cheese in small mixing bowl until light and creamy. Add sifted icing sugar, rind and juice, beating 5 minutes or until mixture is smooth and fluffy.

Cut cake in half horizontally. Spread one third of icing mixture over base half. Sandwich with top layer of cake. Spread remaining icing to completely cover cake. Decorate cake with orange segments and thin strips of rind.

COOK'S FILE

Storage time: 3 days in an airtight container or up to 2 months in the freezer uniced.

RICH CHOCOLATE MUD CAKE

Preparation time: 20 minutes
Cooking time: 2 hours
Makes one 20 cm round cake

1½ cups self-raising flour
½ cup plain flour
⅓ cup cocoa powder
1 tablespoon instant coffee
  powder
250 g unsalted butter
200 g dark chocolate, coarsely
  chopped
1 tablespoon oil
1 cup water
1½ cups caster sugar
2 eggs, lightly beaten

Chocolate Topping
100 g unsalted butter
100 g dark chocolate, chopped

➤ PREHEAT OVEN to moderately slow 160°C. Brush a deep, 20 cm round cake tin with melted butter or oil, line the base and the side with paper; grease paper.

1 Sift the dry ingredients into a large mixing bowl. Make a well in the centre.
Combine butter, chocolate, oil, water and sugar in a medium pan. Stir over low heat until butter and chocolate have melted and sugar has dissolved. Remove from heat.

2 Add butter mixture to the dry ingredients. Stir with a whisk until just combined; add the eggs, mix well; do not overbeat.

3 Pour mixture into prepared tin. Bake 2 hours or until skewer comes out clean when inserted in centre of cake. Leave cake in tin until cold before turning onto wire rack.

4 To make Chocolate Topping: Combine butter and chocolate in a medium pan. Stir over low heat until butter and chocolate have melted and mixture is smooth. Remove from heat. Allow mixture to cool until it becomes spreadable. Spread icing to completely cover cake. Serve wedges of cake with a dollop of crème fraîche, if desired.

COOK'S FILE

Storage time: 2 weeks in an airtight container stored in a cool place or up to 3 months in the freezer uniced.
Variation: Halve the quantity of Chocolate Topping ingredients if you wish to cover the top of the cake only, as shown in the main picture.
Hint: It is important to allow this cake to become cold before turning it out of the tin. If it is hot, it will break apart.

BUTTER CAKES

BASIC BUTTER CAKE

Preparation time: 20 minutes
Cooking time: 45 minutes
Makes one 20 cm round cake

125 g unsalted butter
¾ cup caster sugar
2 eggs, lightly beaten
1 teaspoon imitation vanilla
 essence
2 cups self-raising flour
½ cup milk

Lemon Glacé Icing
1 cup icing sugar
15 g unsalted butter, melted
3-4 teaspoons lemon juice

➤ PREHEAT OVEN to moderate 180°C. Brush a deep, 20 cm round cake tin with melted butter or oil, line base and side with paper; grease paper.

1 Using electric beaters, beat butter and sugar in small mixing bowl until light and creamy.
Add the eggs gradually, beating thoroughly after each addition. Add essence; beat until combined.

2 Transfer the mixture to a large mixing bowl. Using a metal spoon, fold in the sifted flour alternately with the milk. Stir until just combined and the mixture is almost smooth.
Spoon mixture into prepared tin; smooth surface. Bake 45 minutes or until skewer comes out clean when inserted in centre of cake. Leave in tin 10 minutes before turning onto wire rack to cool.

3 To make Lemon Glacé Icing: Combine sifted icing sugar, melted butter and sufficient lemon juice in a small bowl to form a firm paste.
Stand bowl in a pan of simmering water, stirring until icing is smooth and glossy; do not overheat or the icing will be dull and grainy. Remove from heat. Spread icing over cake using a flat-bladed knife.

COOK'S FILE

Storage time: 1 week in an airtight container or up to 3 months in the freezer uniced.
Variation: Add 1 teaspoon lemon rind and 2 teaspoons lemon juice to cake mixture after adding essence.
Hint: Sugar assists in incorporating air into fat, so it is important to use the type of sugar appropriate to the recipe. Caster sugar is ideal for butter cakes because it is superfine; the finer the crystals, the more numerous the air cells and the lighter the finished cake.

RICH BUTTER CAKE

Preparation time: 20 minutes
Cooking time: 45 minutes
Makes one 20 cm round cake

185 g unsalted butter
¾ cup caster sugar
3 eggs, lightly beaten
1 teaspoon imitation vanilla
　essence
1½ cups self-raising flour
½ cup plain flour
¼ cup milk
icing sugar, for decoration

➤ PREHEAT OVEN to moderate 180˚C.
Brush a deep, 20 cm round cake tin with melted butter or oil, line base and side with paper; grease paper.

1 Using electric beaters, beat butter and sugar in small mixing bowl until light and creamy.
Add eggs gradually, beating mixture thoroughly after each addition. Add essence; beat until combined.

2 Transfer mixture to large mixing bowl. Using a metal spoon, fold in sifted flours alternately with milk. Stir until ingredients are just combined and the mixture is almost smooth.

3 Spoon mixture into prepared tin; smooth surface. Bake for 45 minutes or until skewer comes out clean when inserted in centre of cake.
Leave in tin 10 minutes before turning onto wire rack to cool. Dust cake with sifted icing sugar.

COOK'S FILE

Storage time: 1 week in an airtight container or up to 3 months in the freezer uniced.
Hint: If the top of the cake has risen to a peak, or 'tunnels' are visible when you cut it, your oven may be too hot or you may have overmixed the batter.

CHERRY CAKE

Preparation time: 30 minutes
Cooking time: 35 to 40 minutes
Makes one 20 cm ring cake

125 g unsalted butter
¾ cup caster sugar
2 eggs, lightly beaten
½ teaspoon imitation vanilla
   essence
1 cup/265 g glacé cherries,
   chopped
2 cups self-raising flour
½ cup milk

➤ PREHEAT OVEN to moderate 180°C.

1 Brush a deep, 20 cm ring tin with melted butter or oil, line base with paper; grease paper. Using electric beaters, beat butter and sugar in small bowl until light and creamy.

2 Add eggs gradually, beating thoroughly after each addition. Add essence; beat until combined. Transfer mixture to large mixing bowl; add cherries. Using a metal spoon, fold in sifted flour alternately with milk. Stir until just combined and mixture is almost smooth.

3 Spoon the mixture evenly into the prepared tin; smooth surface. Bake for 35 to 40 minutes or until skewer comes out clean when inserted in centre of cake. Leave cake in tin 10 minutes before turning onto wire rack to cool. Dust with sifted icing sugar, if desired.

COOK'S FILE

Storage time: 1 week in an airtight container; up to 2 months in the freezer.
Variation: Add ¾ cup canned pitted cherries, chopped, in place of glacé. Reduce milk to ⅓ cup. Storage time will be only 3 days because of the extra moisture content of the cherries.

1

2

3

SULTANA BARS

Preparation time: 20 minutes
Cooking time: 20 minutes
Makes two bar cakes

125 g unsalted butter
⅔ cup caster sugar
2 eggs, lightly beaten
½ teaspoon imitation vanilla
  essence
1 teaspoon brandy (optional)
¾ cup sultanas or mixed fruit
1¾ cups self-raising flour
⅓ cup milk

➤ PREHEAT OVEN to moderate 180°C.
1 Brush two 26 x 8 x 4.5 cm bar tins with melted butter or oil, line base and sides with paper; grease paper.
Using electric beaters, beat butter and sugar in small mixing bowl until light and creamy.
2 Add eggs gradually, beating thoroughly after each addition. Add the essence and brandy, if used; beat until combined.
Transfer mixture to large mixing bowl; add sultanas. Using a metal spoon, fold in sifted flour alternately with the milk. Stir until the ingredients are just combined and the mixture is almost smooth.
3 Spoon mixture evenly into prepared tins; smooth surface. Bake 20 minutes or until skewer comes out clean when inserted in centre of cakes.
Leave the cakes in tins for 5 minutes before turning them onto a wire rack to cool.

COFFEE BUTTER CAKE

Preparation time: 30 minutes
Cooking time: 35 minutes
Makes one 28 cm oblong cake

150 g unsalted butter
1 cup soft brown sugar
2 eggs, lightly beaten
2 teaspoons instant coffee
  powder
2 cups self-raising flour
½ cup milk

Coffee Butter Cream
100 g unsalted butter
¾ cup icing sugar
2 tablespoons soft brown sugar
2 teaspoons instant coffee powder

➤ PREHEAT OVEN to moderate 180°C. Brush a shallow, 28 x 18 x 3 cm oblong cake tin with melted butter or oil, line base and sides with paper; grease paper.
1 Using electric beaters, beat butter and sugar in small mixing bowl until light and creamy. Add eggs gradually, beating thoroughly after each addition. Add coffee powder; beat until combined. Transfer mixture to large mixing bowl.
2 Using a metal spoon, fold in sifted flour alternately with milk. Stir until just combined and mixture is almost smooth. Pour the mixture evenly into prepared tin; smooth surface. Bake for 35 minutes or until skewer comes out clean when inserted in centre of cake. Leave cake in tin 10 minutes before turning onto wire rack to cool.
3 To make Coffee Butter Cream: Using electric beaters, beat butter in small mixing bowl until light and creamy.
Add sifted icing sugar, brown sugar and coffee powder; beat until mixture is smooth and fluffy. Spread mixture over cake using a flat-bladed knife.

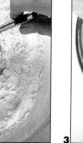

*Opposite: Sultana Bars (top),
Coffee Butter Cake (bottom).*

APPLE CRUMBLE CAKE

Preparation time: 45 minutes
Cooking time: 45 minutes
Makes one 23 cm oblong cake

100 g unsalted butter
1/2 cup caster sugar
1 egg, lightly beaten
1/2 teaspoon imitation vanilla
   essence
1 1/4 cups self-raising flour
1/3 cup milk
1 x 425 g can pie apple,
   roughly chopped
2 tablespoons soft brown sugar
40 g unsalted butter, extra
1/2 cup rolled oats

➤ PREHEAT OVEN to moderate 180°C. Brush a deep, 23 x 13 x 7 cm loaf tin with melted butter or oil, line base and sides with paper; grease the paper.

1 Using electric beaters, beat butter and sugar in a small mixing bowl until light and creamy. Add egg gradually, beating thoroughly after each addition. Add the essence; beat until combined. Transfer the mixture to a large mixing bowl.

2 Using a metal spoon, fold in sifted flour alternately with milk. Stir until just combined and mixture is almost smooth. Spoon mixture into prepared tin; smooth surface. Top with apple. Combine sugar, extra butter and oats in a small pan. Stir over low heat until

sugar has dissolved and butter has melted; remove from heat. Spoon crumble evenly over apple.

3 Bake 45 minutes or until skewer comes out clean when inserted in centre of cake.

Leave cake in tin 15 minutes. Place tin on board. Lift cake out by holding greaseproof paper. Transfer cake to wire rack to cool. Tilt cake to one side, pull away half the paper, repeat with other side. Serve plain or with cream.

COOK'S FILE

Storage time: This cake is best eaten the day it is made.

Variation: Use canned pears in place of apple. Substitute breadcrumbs for the rolled oats.

CHOCOLATE AND STRAWBERRY MARBLE CAKE

Preparation time: 30 minutes
Cooking time: 35 minutes
Makes one 28 cm oblong cake

150 g unsalted butter
3/4 cup caster sugar
2 eggs, lightly beaten
1 teaspoon imitation vanilla
  essence
1 2/3 cups self-raising flour
1/2 cup milk
2 tablespoons cocoa powder
4-5 drops red food colouring
4 drops strawberry-flavoured
  imitation essence or oil

Cream Cheese Icing
100 g cream cheese, softened
3/4 cup icing sugar
1 tablespoon hot milk
1 tablespoon cocoa powder

➤ PREHEAT OVEN to moderate 180°C. Brush a shallow, 28 x 18 x 3 cm oblong cake tin with melted butter or oil, line base and sides with paper; grease paper.

1 Using electric beaters, beat butter and sugar in small mixing bowl until light and creamy. Add eggs gradually, beating thoroughly after each addition. Add essence; beat until combined.

2 Transfer mixture to large mixing bowl. Using a metal spoon, fold in sifted flour alternately with milk. Stir until just combined and the mixture is almost smooth. Divide mixture evenly between two bowls. Add the sifted cocoa powder to one bowl and the colouring and flavoured essence to the other; mix well.

3 Spoon the two mixtures alternately into prepared tin. Swirl mixture in

circles with skewer. Bake cake for 35 minutes or until skewer comes out clean when inserted in centre. Leave cake in tin 10 minutes before turning onto wire rack to cool.

To make Cream Cheese Icing: Using electric beaters, beat cream cheese and sifted icing sugar in a small mixing bowl until light and creamy. Combine the milk and cocoa powder in a small bowl to form a smooth paste. Add cocoa mixture to the cream cheese mixture. Beat until smooth and fluffy. This icing is best used on the day that it is made. Spread over cake using a flat-bladed knife. Cut the cake into squares to serve.

COOK'S FILE

Storage time: 1 week uniced in an airtight container or up to 3 months in the freezer uniced.

Hint: It is not essential to sift cocoa when it is to be mixed with a liquid.

GINGER BUTTER CAKE

Preparation time: 25 minutes
Cooking time: 45 minutes
Makes one 20 cm round cake

125 g unsalted butter
½ cup soft brown sugar
¼ cup caster sugar
2 eggs, lightly beaten
1¾ cups self-raising flour
1 tablespoon ground ginger
½ teaspoon ground cinnamon
¼ teaspoon ground allspice
¼ cup malted milk powder
½ cup ginger beer
glacé or crystallised ginger, for
    decoration

Ginger Lemon Glacé Icing
⅓ cup icing sugar
½ teaspoon ground ginger
20 g unsalted butter, melted
2 teaspoons milk
1 teaspoon lemon juice

➤ PREHEAT OVEN to moderate
180°C.
1 Brush a deep, 20 cm round cake tin
with melted butter or oil, line base and
side with paper; grease paper.
Using electric beaters, beat butter and
sugars in small mixing bowl until light
and creamy. Add the eggs gradually,
beating thoroughly after each addition.

2 Transfer mixture to a large mixing
bowl. Using a metal spoon, fold in the
sifted dry ingredients alternately with
the ginger beer. Stir until just combined and the mixture is almost
smooth.
3 Pour mixture into prepared tin;
smooth surface. Bake 45 minutes or
until a skewer comes out clean when
inserted in centre of cake. Leave cake
in tin 10 minutes before turning onto
wire rack to cool.
**4 To make Ginger Lemon Glacé
Icing:** Combine sifted icing sugar,
ginger, melted butter, milk and lemon
juice in a small bowl to form a paste.
Stand bowl in a pan of simmering
water, stirring until icing is smooth
and glossy; remove from heat.
Spread icing over cake using a flat-
bladed knife. Work quickly, dipping
the knife into hot water occasionally to
give a smooth, shiny finish; do not
reheat icing. Decorate cake with slices
of glacé or crystallised ginger.

COOK'S FILE

Storage time: 1 week in an airtight
container or up to 3 months in the
freezer uniced.
Hint: Glacé fruit is made by soaking
fruit pieces repeatedly in hot syrup,
then coating with a sugar glaze that
becomes flaky when dry. Crystallised
fruits are also dipped in hot syrup, but
are coated in caster sugar to finish.

SAND CAKE

Preparation time: 20 minutes
Cooking time: 45 to 50 minutes
Makes one 23 cm oblong cake

250 g unsalted butter
¾ cup caster sugar
3 eggs, lightly beaten
1 teaspoon imitation vanilla
   essence
2 tablespoons brandy or sherry
1¼ cups self-raising flour
⅔ cup rice flour

➤ PREHEAT OVEN to moderate 180°C. Brush a deep, 23 x 13 x 7 cm loaf tin with melted butter or oil, line base and sides with paper; grease the paper.

1 Using electric beaters, beat butter and sugar in small mixing bowl until light and creamy. Add eggs gradually, beating thoroughly after each addition. Add essence and brandy; beat until combined.

2 Transfer the mixture to a large mixing bowl. Using a metal spoon, fold in sifted flours. Stir until just combined and the mixture is almost smooth. Spoon the mixture into the prepared tin; smooth the surface.

3 Bake for 45 to 50 minutes or until skewer comes out clean when inserted in centre of cake.

Leave cake in tin 10 minutes before turning onto wire rack to cool. Dust with sifted icing sugar, if desired.

COOK'S FILE

Storage time: 3 days in an airtight container or up to 2 months in the freezer.

Variation: Stir 2 tablespoons of lime, lemon, orange or apple juice into the cake mixture in place of the brandy or sherry, if preferred.

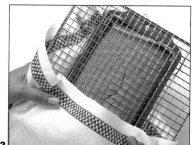

1

2

3

4

FAIRY CAKES

Preparation time: 30 minutes
Cooking time: 10 to 15 minutes
Makes 36 patty cakes

150 g unsalted butter
¾ cup caster sugar
2 eggs, lightly beaten
1 teaspoon imitation vanilla
　essence
2 teaspoons lemon juice
2 cups self-raising flour
½ cup milk
½ cup raspberry jam
1¼ cups cream, whipped
icing sugar, for decoration

➤ PREHEAT OVEN to moderate
180°C.
1 Line two 12 cup, deep patty tins
with paper patty cases.

Using electric beaters, beat butter and
sugar in small mixing bowl until light
and creamy. Add the eggs gradually,
beating thoroughly after each addition.
Add the essence and juice; beat until
combined.
2 Transfer mixture to large mixing
bowl. Using a metal spoon, fold in
sifted flour alternately with milk. Stir
until just combined and the mixture is
almost smooth.
Spoon level tablespoonfuls of mixture
into prepared patty cases. Bake 10 to
15 minutes or until golden. Leave in
tins 5 minutes before placing on wire
rack to cool.
3 Line tins again with patty cases;
repeat the cooking procedure with the
remaining mixture.
When patty cakes are cold, cut out a
small circle from the top of each one,
cutting down to a depth of about 2 cm
to allow for the filling.

4 Spoon ½ teaspoon jam into each
patty cake; top with 1 teaspoon cream.
Place small circle of cake on top. Dust
with sifted icing sugar.

COOK'S FILE

Storage time: 1 week in an airtight
container without the filling or up to
3 months in the freezer unfilled.
Variation: Add ½ cup grated chocolate
to the cake mix when folding in the flour
and the milk.

CARAMEL CREAM CAKE

Preparation time: 30 minutes
Cooking time: 20 minutes
Makes one 20 cm round layer cake

185 g unsalted butter
½ cup soft brown sugar
2 eggs, lightly beaten
¼ cup caramel corn syrup
2 cups self-raising flour
⅓ cup milk

Caramel Cream
¼ cup soft brown sugar
2 tablespoons water
¾ cup cream, whipped
¼ cup flaked almonds, toasted

▶ PREHEAT OVEN to moderate 180°C. Brush two shallow, 20 cm round cake tins with melted butter or oil, line bases and sides with paper; grease paper.

1 Using electric beaters, beat butter and sugar in small mixing bowl until light and creamy. Add eggs gradually, beating thoroughly after each addition. Add the corn syrup and beat until combined.
Transfer mixture to large mixing bowl. Using a metal spoon, stir in sifted flour alternately with milk. Stir until just combined and the mixture is almost smooth.

2 Divide mixture evenly between the two tins. Smooth the surface. Bake for 20 minutes or until skewer comes out clean when inserted in centre of cakes. Leave in tins 5 minutes before turning onto wire rack to cool.

3 To make the Caramel Cream: Combine sugar and water in a small pan. Stir over low heat until sugar has dissolved. Bring to boil. Reduce heat; simmer until liquid has reduced by half. Remove from heat. Cool slightly.

Allow bubbles to subside. Combine cream and sugar mixture in a small bowl. Cover and chill 10 to 15 minutes. Divide cream in half. Spread the base of one cake with cream. Place other cake on top, spread top with remaining cream, sprinkle with almonds.

COOK'S FILE

Storage time: This cake is best prepared and eaten the same day.
Hint: Caramel corn syrup can be bought in your local supermarket in the cake-making section.

ORANGE SYRUP BUTTER CAKE

Preparation time: 45 minutes
Cooking time: 40 minutes
Makes one 20 cm baba cake

150 g unsalted butter
¾ cup caster sugar
2 eggs, lightly beaten
1 teaspoon finely grated orange
   rind
2 cups self-raising flour
¼ cup powdered milk
½ cup orange juice

Orange Syrup
rind of 1 orange
½ cup orange juice
¼ cup caster sugar

➤ PREHEAT OVEN to moderate 180°C.

1 Brush a deep, 20 cm baba tin with melted butter or oil.

Using electric beaters, beat butter and sugar in small mixing bowl until light and creamy. Add eggs gradually, beating thoroughly after each addition. Add rind; beat until combined.

2 Transfer mixture to a large mixing bowl. Using a metal spoon, fold in the sifted dry ingredients alternately with the juice. Stir until just combined and the mixture is almost smooth.

Spoon mixture into prepared tin; smooth surface. Bake 40 minutes or until a skewer comes out clean when inserted in centre of cake. Leave cake in tin 10 minutes before turning onto wire rack to cool.

3 To make Orange Syrup: Slice orange rind into long, thin strips. Combine juice, sugar and rind in small pan. Stir constantly over low heat until the mixture boils and sugar has dissolved. Reduce heat, simmer without stirring, uncovered, for 15 minutes or until reduced by one quarter.

4 Remove from heat. Pour the warm syrup over the warm cake. Serve with freshly whipped cream, if desired.

COOK'S FILE

Storage time: 3 days in an airtight container or 1 month in the freezer.
Hint: 2 medium oranges were used to produce the 1 cup of juice required in the cake and the syrup in this recipe.

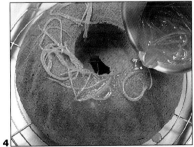

CHOCOLATE BUTTER CAKE

Preparation time: 25 minutes
Cooking time: 45 minutes
Makes one 20 cm round cake

150 g unsalted butter
¾ cup caster sugar
2 eggs, lightly beaten
1 teaspoon imitation vanilla
  essence
1¾ cups self-raising flour
½ cup cocoa powder
¾ cup milk
fresh strawberries, for
  decoration

Chocolate Butter Cream
60 g unsalted butter
⅔ cup icing sugar
2 tablespoons cocoa powder
2 teaspoons milk

➤ PREHEAT OVEN to moderate 180°C. Brush a deep, 20 cm round cake tin with melted butter or oil, line base and side with paper; grease paper.

1 Using electric beaters, beat butter and sugar in small mixing bowl until light and creamy. Add the eggs gradually, beating thoroughly after each addition. Add the essence; beat until combined. Transfer mixture to a large mixing bowl.

2 Using a metal spoon, fold in sifted flour and cocoa powder alternately with milk. Stir until just combined and mixture is almost smooth. Spoon the mixture into the prepared tin; smooth the surface.

3 Bake 45 minutes or until skewer comes out clean when inserted in centre of cake. Leave in tin 10 minutes before turning onto wire rack to cool.

4 To make Chocolate Butter Cream: Beat butter in small mixing bowl until light and creamy. Add sifted icing sugar, cocoa powder and milk, beating 3 minutes or until mixture is smooth and fluffy. Spread icing over cake using a flat-bladed knife. Decorate cake with sliced fresh strawberries.

COOK'S FILE

Storage time: 1 week in an airtight container or up to 3 months in the freezer uniced.

Variation: Use seasonal fruits of your choice for decoration.

PECAN BUTTER CAKE

Preparation time: 25 minutes
Cooking time: 40 minutes
Makes one 20 cm square cake

125 g unsalted butter
½ cup caster sugar
¼ cup raw sugar
2 eggs, lightly beaten
1 teaspoon imitation vanilla
  essence
¾ cup ground pecans
1½ cups self-raising flour
½ cup milk
whole pecans, for decoration

Coffee Icing
1 cup icing sugar
1 teaspoon instant coffee
  powder
1-2 tablespoons water

➤ PREHEAT OVEN to moderate 180°C. Brush a deep, 20 cm square cake tin with melted butter or oil, line base and sides with paper; grease the paper.

1 Using electric beaters, beat butter and sugars in small mixing bowl until light and creamy. Add eggs gradually, beating thoroughly after each addition. Add essence; beat until combined. Transfer mixture to large mixing bowl; add ground pecans.

2 Using a metal spoon, fold in sifted flour alternately with the milk. Stir until just combined and the mixture is almost smooth.

Pour mixture into prepared tin; smooth surface. Bake 40 minutes or until skewer comes out clean when inserted in centre of cake. Leave cake in tin 10 minutes before turning onto wire rack to cool.

3 To make Coffee Icing: Combine sifted icing sugar, coffee and sufficient liquid in a small bowl to form a firm paste. Stand bowl in pan of simmering water, stirring until icing is smooth and glossy; remove from heat. Spread icing over cake using a flat-bladed knife. Decorate with whole pecans.

COOK'S FILE

Storage time: 1 week in an airtight container or up to 3 months in the freezer uniced.
Variation: Use nuts of your choice.

1

2

3

FRUIT AND VEGETABLE CAKES

ZUCCHINI AND RAISIN CAKE

Preparation time: 15 minutes
Cooking time: 35 to 40 minutes
Makes one 20 cm baba cake

125 g unsalted butter
2/3 cup caster sugar
2 eggs, lightly beaten
2 teaspoons imitation vanilla
  essence
1 1/2 cups coarsely grated
  zucchini
1/3 cup finely chopped raisins
1 1/2 cups self-raising flour

Vanilla Butter Cream
1/2 cup caster sugar
1/3 cup water
125 g unsalted butter
2 teaspoons imitation vanilla
  essence

➤ PREHEAT OVEN to moderate 180°C. Brush a deep, 20 cm baba tin with melted butter or oil.

1 Using electric beaters, beat butter and sugar in small mixing bowl until light and creamy. Add eggs gradually, beating the mixture thoroughly after each addition. Add the essence; beat until just combined.

2 Transfer mixture to large mixing bowl; add zucchini and raisins. Using a metal spoon, fold in sifted flour; stir until just combined and the mixture is almost smooth. Spoon evenly into the prepared tin; smooth surface. Bake for 35 to 40 minutes or until skewer comes out clean when inserted in centre of cake. Leave cake in tin for 10 minutes before turning onto wire rack to cool.

3 To make Vanilla Butter Cream: Combine sugar and water in small pan. Stir constantly over low heat until the mixture boils and sugar has dissolved. Reduce heat, simmer without stirring, uncovered, 5 minutes. Remove from heat; cool. Using electric beaters, beat butter and essence in small mixing bowl until light and creamy.

Pour syrup onto creamed mixture, beating until all has been added and mixture is smooth and fluffy. Spread top and sides of cake with mixture.

COOK'S FILE

Storage time: 3 days in an airtight container in the refrigerator or up to 2 months in the freezer uniced.

BANANA PEANUT BUTTER CAKE

Preparation time: 10 minutes
Cooking time: 1 hour
Makes one 21 cm oblong cake

125 g unsalted butter
½ cup soft brown sugar
¼ cup honey
2 eggs, lightly beaten
⅓ cup crunchy peanut butter
1 cup mashed banana
2 cups wholemeal self-raising flour

➤ PREHEAT OVEN to moderate 180˚C. Brush a deep, 21 x 14 x 7 cm loaf tin with melted butter or oil. Line the base and sides with paper; grease the paper.

1 Using electric beaters, beat butter, sugar and honey in small mixing bowl until light and creamy. Add eggs gradually, beating thoroughly after each addition. Add peanut butter; beat until combined.

2 Transfer mixture to large mixing bowl; add banana. Using a metal spoon, fold in sifted flour, including husks. Stir until just combined and the mixture is almost smooth.

3 Spoon mixture into prepared tin; smooth surface. Bake 1 hour or until skewer comes out clean when inserted in centre of cake. Leave cake in tin for 10 minutes before turning onto a wire rack to cool. Serve sliced and spread with butter, if desired.

COOK'S FILE

Storage time: Up to 1 week in an airtight container in the refrigerator and 1 month in the freezer.
Hint: Use soft, very ripe bananas for this cake. Mash them with a fork; do not liquidise them in a food processor or they will add too much moisture.

SOUR CREAM PRUNE CAKE

Preparation time: 15 minutes
Cooking time: 35 minutes
Makes one 20 cm baba cake

60 g unsalted butter
60 g cream cheese, softened
2/3 cup caster sugar
1 egg, lightly beaten
2 teaspoons finely grated lemon
   rind
1/3 cup sour cream
1/2 cup chopped prunes
1 1/3 cups self-raising flour

➤ PREHEAT OVEN to moderate 180°C.

1 Brush a deep, 20 cm baba tin with melted butter or oil.
Using electric beaters, beat butter, cheese and sugar in small mixing bowl until light and creamy.

2 Add the egg gradually, beating thoroughly after each addition. Add the rind and the sour cream; beat until just combined.

3 Transfer mixture to a large mixing bowl; add prunes. Using a metal spoon, fold in sifted flour. Stir until mixture is almost smooth.
Pour mixture evenly into prepared tin; smooth surface. Bake 35 minutes or until skewer comes out clean when inserted in centre of cake. Leave cake in tin for 10 minutes before turning onto a wire rack to cool.

COOK'S FILE

Storage time: 3 days in an airtight container in the refrigerator or up to 2 months in the freezer.

Hint: Do not overbeat cake mixture once the sour cream has been added. Overbeating with electric beaters may produce a heavy-textured cake.

1

2

3

ZUCCHINI AND APRICOT LOAF

Preparation time: 20 minutes
Cooking time: 50 to 55 minutes
Makes one 25 cm oblong cake

100 g unsalted butter
1/2 cup caster sugar
2 eggs, lightly beaten
1 teaspoon finely grated lemon rind
1 1/2 cups coarsely grated zucchini
2 tablespoons finely chopped dried apricots
3/4 cup wholemeal self-raising flour
1/2 cup self-raising flour
2 tablespoons milk

Creamy Apricot Topping
1/3 cup finely chopped dried apricots
1/2 cup water
100 g cream cheese, softened
2 tablespoons icing sugar

➤ PREHEAT OVEN to moderate 180°C. Brush a 25 x 15 x 5.5 cm loaf tin with melted butter or oil. Line base and sides with paper; grease paper.
1 Using electric beaters, beat butter and sugar in small mixing bowl until light and creamy. Add eggs gradually, beating thoroughly after each addition. Add rind, beat until combined.
2 Transfer mixture to large mixing bowl; add zucchini and apricots. Using a metal spoon, fold in sifted flours, including husks, alternately with milk. Stir until just combined and the mixture is almost smooth. Pour into prepared tin; smooth surface.
Bake 50 to 55 minutes or until skewer comes out clean when inserted in the centre of the cake. Leave cake in tin for

10 minutes before turning onto wire rack to cool.
3 To make the Creamy Apricot Topping: Combine apricots and water in small pan. Stir over high heat until mixture boils. Reduce heat, simmer without stirring, uncovered, for 10 minutes or until almost all liquid is absorbed and the apricots are soft. Remove from heat; cool completely. Using electric beaters, beat cheese and

sifted icing sugar in small mixing bowl until light and creamy. Add the undrained apricot pulp, beating for 2 minutes or until the mixture is almost smooth and is fluffy. Spread sides and top of cake with mixture.

COOK'S FILE

Storage time: 3 days in an airtight container in the refrigerator or up to 2 months in the freezer uniced.

1

2

3

QUICK AND EASY CARROT CAKE

Preparation time: 15 minutes
Cooking time: 45 minutes
Makes one 23 cm square cake

1 cup vegetable oil
3 eggs, lightly beaten
1 cup caster sugar
3 cups coarsely grated carrot
⅓ cup crushed pineapple, well
    drained
2 tablespoons sultanas

2 teaspoons mixed spice
1¼ cups self-raising flour
1 cup wholemeal self-raising
    flour

➤ PREHEAT OVEN to moderate 180°C. Brush a deep, 23 cm square cake tin with melted butter or oil. Line the base and sides with paper; grease the paper.

1 Using electric beaters, beat oil, eggs and sugar in small mixing bowl until light and creamy.

2 Transfer mixture to large mixing bowl; add carrot and fruits. Using a metal spoon, fold in the sifted dry ingredients, including husks; stir until just combined.

3 Pour mixture evenly into prepared tin; smooth surface. Bake 45 minutes or until skewer comes out clean when inserted in centre of cake. Leave cake in tin 10 minutes before turning onto wire rack to cool. Serve dusted with sifted icing sugar, if desired.

COOK'S FILE

Storage time: 3 days in an airtight container in the refrigerator or up to 2 months in the freezer.

ORANGE AND SPICE PUMPKIN CAKE

Preparation time: 30 minutes
Cooking time: 45 minutes
Makes one 20 cm round cake

1⅔ cups plain flour
1 teaspoon bicarbonate of soda
½ teaspoon ground nutmeg
½ teaspoon ground ginger
½ teaspoon ground cinnamon
125 g unsalted butter
⅔ cup honey
1 egg, lightly beaten
1 tablespoon finely grated
   orange rind
1 cup/400 g mashed pumpkin,
   well drained
1 cup rolled oats

Orange Cream
125 g cream cheese, softened
½ cup icing sugar
2 teaspoons finely grated
   orange rind
1 tablespoon orange juice

➤ PREHEAT OVEN to moderate 180°C. Brush a deep, 20 cm round cake tin with melted butter or oil. Line base and side with paper; grease paper.
1 Place flour, soda and spices in a food-processor bowl; add butter. Using the pulse action, press the button for 15 seconds or until mixture is a fine crumbly texture.
2 Add honey, egg, rind and pumpkin to bowl, process 10 seconds until the ingredients are just combined. Transfer mixture to a large mixing bowl. Using a metal spoon, fold in the oats.
3 Pour mixture into prepared tin; smooth surface. Bake 45 minutes or until a skewer comes out clean when inserted in centre of cake. Leave cake

in tin 10 minutes before turning onto wire rack to cool.
To make Orange Cream: Using electric beaters, beat cheese and sifted icing sugar in small mixing bowl until light and creamy. Add the rind and juice, beat 3 minutes or until mixture

is smooth and fluffy. Spread over top of cake using a flat-bladed knife.

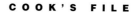
COOK'S FILE

Storage time: 3 days in an airtight container in the refrigerator or up to 2 months in the freezer uniced.

1

2

3

PINEAPPLE COCONUT CAKE

Preparation time: 15 minutes
Cooking time: 45 minutes
Makes one 20 cm baba cake

2 tablespoons desiccated
   coconut
2/3 cup vegetable oil
3 eggs, lightly beaten
2/3 cup caster sugar
2 teaspoons imitation vanilla
   essence
2/3 cup unsweetened crushed
   pineapple, well drained
1 cup desiccated coconut, extra
2 cups self-raising flour
2 tablespoons milk
toasted shredded coconut,
   optional, for decoration

Pineapple Icing
1 1/2 cups icing sugar
2 tablespoons pineapple juice
2 teaspoons unsalted butter

➤ PREHEAT OVEN to moderate 180°C. Brush a deep, 20 cm baba tin with melted butter or oil. Coat base and sides evenly with desiccated coconut; shake off excess.

1 Using electric beaters, beat the oil, eggs, sugar and the essence in a small mixing bowl at high speed for 3 minutes or until mixture is thick and increased in volume.

2 Transfer mixture to large mixing bowl; add pineapple and coconut. Using a metal spoon, fold in the sifted flour alternately with the milk. Stir until just combined and the mixture is almost smooth. Spoon mixture evenly into prepared tin; smooth the surface.

Bake for 45 minutes or until skewer comes out clean when inserted in the centre. Leave the cake in the tin for 5 minutes before turning it onto a wire rack to cool.

3 To make Pineapple Icing: Combine sifted icing sugar, juice and butter in a small heatproof bowl. Stand bowl in a pan of simmering water, stirring mixture until the butter has melted and the icing is glossy and smooth. Cool slightly.

Using a spoon, drizzle the icing over the top of the cake, allowing it to run freely down the sides. Scatter the toasted, shredded coconut over the cake, if using.

COOK'S FILE

Storage time: 3 days in an airtight container in the refrigerator or up to 2 months in the freezer uniced.

1

2

3

LAYERED CARAMEL BANANA CAKE

Preparation time: 20 minutes
Cooking time: 45 minutes
Makes one 20 cm round cake

100 g unsalted butter
½ cup caster sugar
1 egg, lightly beaten
1 cup mashed banana
2 cups self-raising flour
⅓ cup golden syrup
½ teaspoon ground
    cinnamon
⅔ cup flaked almonds

➤ PREHEAT OVEN to moderate 180°C.
Brush a round, 20 cm springform tin with melted butter or oil. Line base with paper; grease paper.
1 Using electric beaters, beat butter and sugar in small mixing bowl until light and creamy. Add egg gradually, beating thoroughly after each addition. Transfer the mixture to a large mixing bowl; add banana.
2 Using a metal spoon, fold in sifted flour. Stir until just combined. Reserve ⅔ cup of the mixture.
Spoon the remaining mixture evenly into the prepared tin; smooth surface. Bake for 25 minutes.

3 Combine syrup, cinnamon, almonds and the reserved cake mixture in a small bowl.
Spoon mixture over partly cooked cake; smooth surface. Return the cake to the oven, cook a further 20 minutes or until skewer comes out clean when inserted in centre of cake. Cool cake in tin. Dust with sifted icing sugar to serve, if desired.

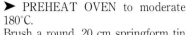

COOK'S FILE

Storage time: 2 days in an airtight container in the refrigerator.
Hint: Use a hot spoon for measuring out the golden syrup; this will help it flow freely into the measuring cup.

PINEAPPLE PECAN CAKE

Preparation time: 10 minutes
Cooking time: 35 minutes
Makes one 20 cm round cake

80 g unsalted butter
½ cup caster sugar
2 eggs, lightly beaten
⅓ cup finely chopped glacé
    pineapple
2 tablespoons finely chopped
    pecan nuts
1 cup self-raising flour
2 tablespoons custard powder
2 tablespoons milk

➤ PREHEAT OVEN to moderate 180°C. Brush a deep, 20 cm round cake tin with melted butter or oil. Line base with paper; grease paper.
1 Using electric beaters, beat butter and sugar in small mixing bowl at medium speed until light and creamy. Add eggs, beat for 3 minutes or until just combined.
2 Add pineapple, nuts, sifted flour and custard powder and milk. Beat at low speed 1 minute, until almost smooth.
3 Pour mixture evenly into prepared tin; smooth surface. Bake 35 minutes or until skewer comes out clean when inserted in centre of cake. Leave cake in the tin for 5 minutes before turning

onto a wire rack to cool. Dust with icing sugar before serving, if desired.

COOK'S FILE

Storage time: 3 days in an airtight container in the refrigerator or up to 2 months in the freezer uniced.
Hint: Walnuts and pecans are both rich in oil and similar in texture and are interchangeable in most recipes. Hazelnuts and almonds, which are harder than walnuts and pecans, can also be substituted for each other. Keep stored in an airtight container.
The addition of custard powder will give the cake a pleasing appearance and enrich the flavour.

*Opposite: Layered Caramel Banana Cake (top),
Pineapple Pecan Cake (bottom).*

CARROT CAKE WITH BUTTERSCOTCH FROSTING

Preparation time: 25 minutes
Cooking time: 30 minutes
Makes one shallow 28 cm oblong cake

125 g unsalted butter
1/2 cup soft brown sugar
2 eggs, lightly beaten
2 teaspoons finely grated
    orange rind
1 1/2 cups finely grated carrot
2/3 cup chopped walnuts
1 teaspoon ground cinnamon
1/2 teaspoon ground nutmeg
1/4 teaspoon ground cloves
1 1/2 cups self-raising flour
1 cup plain flour
1/4 cup milk

Butterscotch Frosting
20 g unsalted butter
1/2 cup soft brown sugar
1/3 cup sour cream
100 g cream cheese, softened

➤ PREHEAT OVEN to moderate 180°C.
1 Brush a shallow, 28 x 18 x 3 cm oblong cake tin with melted butter or oil. Line base and sides with paper; grease the paper.
Using electric beaters, beat butter and sugar in small mixing bowl until light and creamy. Add the eggs gradually, beating thoroughly after each addition. Add rind, beat until combined.
2 Transfer mixture to large mixing bowl. Add carrot and walnuts. Using a metal spoon, fold in sifted spices and flours alternately with the milk. Spoon mixture evenly into the prepared tin;

smooth surface. Bake 30 minutes or until skewer comes out clean when inserted in centre. Leave 10 minutes before turning onto a wire rack to cool.
3 To make Butterscotch Frosting: Combine butter and sugar in a small pan. Stir constantly over low heat until mixture boils and sugar dissolves. Simmer for 3 minutes, uncovered, stirring occasionally. Remove from heat, add sour cream. Stir until combined; cool. Using electric beaters, beat cheese in a small mixing bowl until light and creamy. Add cooled butterscotch mixture gradually, beating thoroughly after each addition. Spread frosting over cake using a flat-bladed knife.

COOK'S FILE

Storage time: 3 days in an airtight container in the refrigerator or up to 2 months in the freezer uniced.

1   **2**   **3**

APPLE AND WALNUT CAKE

Preparation time: 15 minutes
Cooking time: 40 minutes
Makes one 20 cm round cake

125 g unsalted butter
1 cup icing sugar
2 eggs, lightly beaten
⅟₂ cup chopped walnuts
1⅟₃ cups plain flour
⅟₃ cup custard powder
1 teaspoon baking powder
⅟₂ teaspoon bicarbonate of soda
2 apples, peeled and cored
2 tablespoons apricot jam
2 teaspoons brandy

➤ PREHEAT OVEN to moderate 180°C.

1 Brush a deep, 20 cm round springform tin with melted butter or oil. Line base with paper; grease paper.

2 Using electric beaters, beat butter and sifted icing sugar in small mixing bowl until creamy and white. Add eggs gradually, beating thoroughly after each addition.

Transfer mixture to a large mixing bowl; add walnuts. Using a metal spoon, fold in sifted dry ingredients. Stir until just combined and mixture is almost smooth.

3 Spoon the mixture evenly into prepared tin; smooth the surface. Cut each apple into quarters, then into thin slices lengthways. Arrange apples decoratively over top of cake. Bake 40 minutes or until skewer comes out clean when inserted in centre.

4 Combine jam and brandy in small pan. Stir over low heat until mixture boils. Remove from heat, strain into small bowl. Brush warm jam mixture over hot cake. Cool cake in tin.

COOK'S FILE

Storage time: This cake is best eaten on the day it is made.

TEACAKES

BROWNED BUTTER AND CINNAMON TEACAKE

Preparation time: 35 minutes
Cooking time: 40 minutes
Makes one 20 cm square cake

150 g unsalted butter
1½ cups self-raising flour
¼ cup cornflour
1 teaspoon ground cinnamon
¾ cup caster sugar
3 eggs, lightly beaten
1 teaspoon imitation vanilla
    essence
¼ cup orange juice
¼ cup milk

Browned Cinnamon Icing
30 g unsalted butter
50 g unsalted butter, extra
⅓ cup icing sugar
½ teaspoon ground cinnamon
extra ground cinnamon, for
    decoration

➤ PREHEAT OVEN to moderate 180°C. Brush a deep, 20 cm square cake tin with melted butter or oil, line base and sides with paper; grease paper.
1 Place the butter in a small pan. Stir over low heat until melted. Continue to heat the butter until it turns golden brown. This process should take about 6 minutes. Skim fat solids from the surface. Remove from heat.
2 Sift flours and cinnamon into large mixing bowl. Add the sugar.
Pour the combined eggs, essence, juice, milk and browned butter onto the dry ingredients; using electric beaters, beat on low speed for 3 minutes until just moistened. Beat mixture on high speed 5 minutes or until it is free of lumps and increased in volume.
3 Pour mixture into prepared tin; smooth the surface. Bake 40 minutes or until skewer comes out clean when inserted in centre of cake. Leave cake in tin 10 minutes before turning onto wire rack to cool.
To make Browned Cinnamon Icing: Brown the 30 g butter as for Step 1. Using electric beaters, beat extra butter and sifted icing sugar in small mixing bowl until light and creamy. Add cinnamon and browned butter, beating 2 minutes or until the mixture is smooth and fluffy. Spread the icing over the cake using a flat-bladed knife. Sprinkle with the extra ground cinnamon.

COOK'S FILE

Storage time: 4 days in an airtight container or up to 3 months in the freezer uniced.
Variation: The icing can be made without browned butter, if preferred.

QUICK AND EASY ORANGE TEACAKE

Preparation time: 10 minutes
Cooking time: 25 minutes
Makes one 20 cm ring cake

1⅓ cups wholemeal self-raising
  flour
125 g unsalted butter, chopped
1 tablespoon finely grated
  orange rind
½ cup caster sugar
3 eggs, lightly beaten
2 tablespoons milk

➤ PREHEAT OVEN to moderate 180°C. Brush a 20 cm ring tin with melted butter or oil. Line base with paper; grease paper.

1 Place flour in food-processor bowl; add the butter, rind and sugar. Using the pulse action, press the button for 20 seconds or until mixture is a fine, crumbly texture.

2 Add combined eggs and milk to bowl, process 10 seconds or until mixture is smooth.

3 Spoon mixture into prepared tin; smooth surface. Bake 25 minutes or until skewer comes out clean when inserted in centre of cake.

Leave cake in tin 3 minutes before turning onto wire rack to cool.

COOK'S FILE

Storage time: This cake is best eaten on the day it is made.

Variation: If a food processor is unavailable, this cake can be made successfully with an electric mixer by creaming the butter, rind, sugar and eggs, then folding in the milk and sifted flour (including the husks).

Hint: Be careful when grating the rind of citrus fruits that you do not go too deeply into the skin; the white pith is bitter and should be avoided.

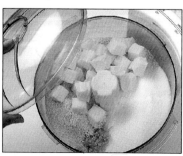

1

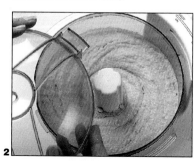

2

3

POPPY SEED CAKE WITH LEMON SYRUP

Preparation time: 40 minutes
Cooking time: 25 to 30 minutes
Makes one 20 cm baba cake

1¾ cups self-raising flour
2 tablespoons poppy seeds
185 g unsalted butter
⅔ cup caster sugar
2 tablespoons apricot jam
1 teaspoon finely grated lemon
    rind
¼ cup lemon juice
2 eggs, lightly beaten

Lemon Syrup
½ cup caster sugar
¼ cup lemon juice
½ cup water

➤ PREHEAT OVEN to moderate 180°C. Brush a deep, 20 cm baba tin with melted butter or oil.

1 Sift flour into large mixing bowl. Add the poppy seeds. Make a well in the centre.
Combine butter, sugar, jam, rind and juice in a medium pan. Stir over low heat until butter has melted and sugar has dissolved; remove from heat.

2 Add the butter mixture to the dry ingredients. Using a whisk, stir until just combined; add eggs, mix well; do not overbeat.
Pour mixture into prepared tin; smooth surface. Bake 25 to 30 minutes or until skewer comes out clean when inserted in centre of cake.

3 To make Lemon Syrup: Combine sugar, juice and water in medium pan. Stir constantly over low heat until mixture boils and sugar has dissolved. Reduce heat, simmer without stirring, uncovered, until mixture has thickened and has reduced by one third. Remove from heat, leave 2 minutes for bubbles to subside.
Pour hot syrup over warm cake in tin. Leave until all syrup is absorbed. Turn onto plate. Serve warm with cream.

COOK'S FILE

Storage time: This cake is best eaten the day it is made. Serve warm to fully appreciate the flavour of the syrup.

HONEY AND COCONUT CAKE

Preparation time: 40 minutes
Cooking time: 30 minutes
Makes one 28 cm oblong cake

125 g unsalted butter
⅔ cup raw sugar
2 eggs, lightly beaten
1 teaspoon imitation vanilla
    essence
¼ cup honey
¼ cup desiccated coconut
1¾ cups self-raising flour
1 teaspoon ground nutmeg
¼ teaspoon ground cinnamon
¼ teaspoon ground allspice
½ cup milk
extra ground nutmeg, for
    decoration

Honey and Cream Cheese Icing
125 g cream cheese, softened
½ cup icing sugar
1 tablespoon honey

➤ PREHEAT OVEN to moderate 180°C. Brush a shallow, 28 x 18 x 3 cm oblong cake tin with melted butter or oil, line base and sides with paper; grease paper.

1 Using electric beaters, beat butter and sugar in small mixing bowl until light and creamy. Add eggs gradually, beating thoroughly after each addition. Add essence and honey; beat until combined.

2 Transfer mixture to large mixing bowl; add coconut. Using a metal spoon, fold in sifted flour and spices alternately with milk. Stir until just combined and the mixture is almost smooth. Pour mixture into prepared tin; smooth surface.

3 Bake 30 minutes or until skewer comes out clean when inserted in the

centre of cake. Leave cake in the tin for 10 minutes before turning onto wire rack to cool.

To make Honey and Cream Cheese Icing: Using electric beaters, beat cream cheese in small mixing bowl until creamy. Add sifted icing sugar and the honey, beating 3 minutes or until mix-

ture is smooth and fluffy. Spread the icing over cake using a flat-bladed knife. Sprinkle with extra nutmeg.

COOK'S FILE

Storage time: 4 days in an airtight container or up to 2 months in the freezer uniced.

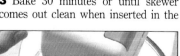

LEMON BUTTER TEACAKE

Preparation time: 10 minutes
Cooking time: 30 minutes
Makes one 20 cm round cake

50 g unsalted butter
80 g cream cheese, softened
¼ cup honey
2 tablespoons prepared lemon
   butter
2 eggs, lightly beaten
1½ cups self-raising flour
¼ cup milk

Lemon Cream Cheese Topping
100 g cream cheese, softened
⅓ cup sour cream
2 tablespoons prepared lemon
   butter, extra

➤ PREHEAT OVEN to moderate 180°C. Brush a shallow, 20 cm round cake tin with melted butter or oil. Line base with paper; grease paper.
1 Using electric beaters, beat butter, cream cheese, honey and lemon butter in small mixing bowl at medium speed until light and creamy. Add eggs, beat 1 minute or until just combined.
2 Add flour and milk, beat at low speed 1 minute or until mixture is smooth. Pour mixture evenly into prepared tin; smooth surface. Bake for 30 minutes or until skewer comes out clean when inserted in centre of cake.
3 Leave cake in tin 5 minutes before turning onto wire rack to cool.
To make Lemon Cream Cheese Topping: Beat cream cheese, sour cream and lemon butter in small mixing bowl until light and creamy. Spread over cake using flat-bladed knife.

COOK'S FILE

Storage time: This cake is best eaten on the day it is made.

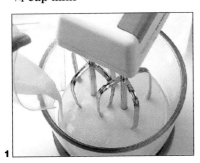

APPLE AND CINNAMON TEACAKE

Preparation time: 15 minutes
Cooking time: 30 minutes
Makes one 20 cm round cake

60 g unsalted butter
⅓ cup caster sugar
½ teaspoon ground cinnamon
1 egg, lightly beaten
½ cup pie apple, chopped
1¼ cups self-raising flour
¼ cup milk

Cinnamon Icing
1 tablespoon water
15 g unsalted butter
¼ cup caster sugar
½ teaspoon ground cinnamon

➤ PREHEAT OVEN to moderate 180°C. Brush a 20 cm round springform tin with melted butter or oil. Line base and side with paper; grease paper.

1 Using electric beaters, beat butter, sugar and cinnamon in small mixing bowl at medium speed until light and creamy. Add egg, beat 1 minute or until just combined.

2 Add the apple, sifted flour and milk. Beat at low speed for 1 minute or until mixture is almost smooth.
Pour mixture evenly into prepared tin; smooth surface. Bake 30 minutes or until skewer comes out clean when inserted in centre of cake.

3 Leave cake in tin 10 minutes before turning onto wire rack to cool.
To make Cinnamon Icing: Combine all the ingredients in a small pan.
Stir constantly over low heat until mixture boils and sugar has dissolved. Simmer without stirring, uncovered, for 2 minutes. Using a flat-bladed knife, spread the warm icing over the top of the warm cake.

COOK'S FILE

Storage time: This cake is best eaten on the day it is made.

Variation: Substitute ground mixed spice for cinnamon in cake and icing. This cake can be served as a dessert with whipped cream.

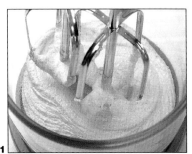

CARDAMOM APPLE CAKE

Preparation time: 30 minutes
Cooking time: 55 minutes
Makes one 20 cm round cake

2 green apples, peeled, cored
¼ cup soft brown sugar
150 g unsalted butter
¾ cup caster sugar
2 eggs, lightly beaten
1 teaspoon imitation vanilla
    essence
2 cups self-raising flour
2 teaspoons ground cardamom
½ cup milk

➤ PREHEAT OVEN to moderate 180°C. Brush a deep, 20 cm round cake tin with melted butter or oil, line base and side with paper; grease paper.

1 Slice one apple in thin rings and finely chop the other one. Place rings of apple in the base of cake tin, overlapping each piece. Sprinkle with brown sugar.

2 Using electric beaters, beat butter and sugar in small mixing bowl until light and creamy. Add eggs gradually, beating thoroughly after each addition. Add essence; beat until combined. Transfer mixture to large mixing bowl; add chopped apple.

3 Using a metal spoon, fold in the sifted flour and the cardamom alternately with the milk. Stir until just combined and the mixture is almost smooth.

Spoon mixture into prepared tin; smooth surface. Bake 55 minutes or until skewer comes out clean when inserted in centre of cake.

Leave cake in tin 20 minutes before turning onto wire rack to cool.

COOK'S FILE

Storage time: This cake is best eaten the day it is made.

Variation: Decorate the top of the cake with strips of glacé or crystallised fruit or ginger, if desired.

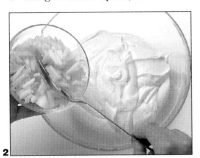

TREACLE GINGER LOAF

Preparation time: 25 minutes
Cooking time: 40 minutes
Makes one 21 cm oblong cake

100 g unsalted butter
½ cup caster sugar
¼ cup soft dark brown sugar
2 eggs, lightly beaten
¼ cup black treacle
⅔ cup self-raising flour
½ cup plain flour
1 tablespoon ground ginger
¼ cup milk
icing sugar, for decoration

➤ PREHEAT OVEN to moderate 180°C. Brush a deep, 21 x 14 x 7 cm loaf tin with melted butter or oil, line base and sides with paper; grease paper.

1 Using electric beaters, beat butter and sugars in small mixing bowl until light and creamy. Add eggs gradually, beating thoroughly after each addition. Add treacle; beat until combined.

2 Transfer mixture to large mixing bowl. Using a metal spoon, fold in the sifted flours and ginger alternately with the milk.

3 Pour mixture into prepared tin; smooth surface.

Bake 40 minutes or until skewer comes out clean when inserted in centre of cake. Leave cake in tin 20 minutes before turning onto wire rack to cool. Dust cake with sifted icing sugar.

COOK'S FILE

Storage time: 1 week in an airtight container or up to 3 months in the freezer.

Variation: Use golden syrup instead of treacle. Treacle has a richer flavour; it is a molasses-like sugar syrup used in toffees and old-fashioned desserts.

1

2

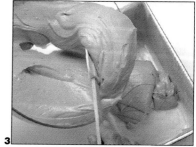

3

CHERRY TEACAKE

Preparation time: 15 minutes
Cooking time: 30 minutes
Makes one 20 cm round cake

60 g unsalted butter
²⁄₃ cup caster sugar
½ teaspoon coconut essence
3 eggs, lightly beaten
⅓ cup chopped glacé cherries
¼ cup desiccated coconut
1¼ cups self-raising flour
⅓ cup cornflour

Pink Icing
½ cup icing sugar

1 teaspoon unsalted butter
2 teaspoons boiling water
pink food colouring

➤ PREHEAT OVEN to moderate 180˚C.
1 Brush a deep, 20 cm round cake tin with melted butter or oil. Line base with paper; grease paper.
Using electric beaters, beat butter, sugar and essence in small mixing bowl at medium speed until light and creamy.
2 Add eggs, beat 3 minutes or until just combined. Transfer the mixture to a large mixing bowl. Add cherries and coconut and sifted flour and cornflour, beat at low speed for 1 minute or until

mixture is almost smooth. Spoon mixture evenly into prepared tin; smooth surface. Bake 30 minutes or until skewer comes out clean when inserted in centre. Leave cake in tin 10 minutes before turning onto wire rack to cool.
3 To make Pink Icing: Combine sifted icing sugar, butter and water in a small bowl to form a firm paste. Stand bowl in pan of simmering water, stir until icing is smooth and glossy; remove from heat. Tint icing with colouring as desired. Spread icing over top of cake using a flat-bladed knife.

COOK'S FILE

Storage time: This cake is best eaten on the day it is made.

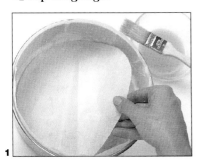

DATE AND WALNUT LOAF

Preparation time: 25 minutes
Cooking time: 1 hour
Makes one 21 cm oblong cake

125 g unsalted butter
½ cup honey
¼ cup soft brown sugar
2 tablespoons milk
1½ cups finely chopped dates
1 teaspoon bicarbonate of soda
2 cups plain flour
½ teaspoon ground nutmeg
1 cup chopped walnuts
2 eggs, lightly beaten

➤ PREHEAT OVEN to moderate 180°C.
1 Brush a deep, 21 x 14 x 7 cm loaf tin with melted butter or oil.
Line base and two sides of tin with paper; grease paper.
2 Combine butter, honey, sugar and milk in a medium pan. Stir over low heat until butter has melted and sugar has dissolved; remove from heat.
Add dates and soda; stir, set aside to cool. Sift flour with nutmeg into large mixing bowl. Add the walnuts. Make a well in the centre.
3 Add butter mixture and eggs to dry ingredients. Using a wooden spoon, stir until well combined; do not overbeat.

Pour mixture evenly into prepared tin; smooth surface. Bake 1 hour or until skewer comes out clean when inserted in centre of cake.
Leave loaf in tin 10 minutes before turning onto wire rack to cool. Serve loaf with butter if desired.

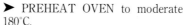
COOK'S FILE

Storage time: This cake is best eaten on the day it is made.
Hint: Honey is useful for its flavour and keeping properties. Cakes made with honey stay moist longer than those made with sugar. The flavour of the honey is determined by the kind of flower the bees have visited.

VANILLA CURRANT TWIST

Preparation time: 15 minutes
Cooking time: 40 minutes
Makes one 26 cm bar cake

1 cup self-raising flour
½ cup plain flour
30 g unsalted butter, chopped
¼ cup caster sugar
¼ cup currants
1 egg
2 tablespoons milk
1½ teaspoons vanilla essence
1 teaspoon milk, extra
icing sugar, for decoration

➤ PREHEAT OVEN to moderate
180°C.
1 Brush a 26 x 8 x 4.5 cm bar tin with
melted butter or oil. Line base and two
sides with paper; grease paper.
Sift flours into large mixing bowl; add
chopped butter and sugar.
Using fingertips, rub butter into flour
for 2 minutes or until the mixture is a
fine, crumbly texture.
2 Add currants; stir. Add combined
egg, milk and essence to bowl, stir to
form a soft, sticky dough.
Turn the mixture onto a lightly floured
surface, knead quickly 1 minute or
until smooth.
3 Form dough into a 50-cm long log.
Fold log in half and twist.
Place twist in prepared tin; brush the
surface with the extra milk. Bake for
40 minutes or until skewer comes out
clean when inserted in centre. Invert
twist onto wire rack to cool.
Dust the twist with sifted icing sugar
just before serving.

COOK'S FILE

Storage time: This cake is best eaten
on the day it is made.

TRADITIONAL FRUIT CAKES

WHOLEMEAL FRUIT AND NUT CAKE

Preparation time: 45 minutes
Cooking time: 2 hours 30 minutes
   to 3 hours
Makes one 20 cm square cake

180 g unsalted butter
¾ cup soft dark brown sugar
3 eggs, lightly beaten
200 g figs, chopped
1 cup/200 g dried apricots,
   chopped
⅔ cup/100 g currants
½ cup/100 g sultanas
1 cup/100 g walnut pieces
½ cup sunflower kernels
1½ cups plain wholemeal flour
½ cup self-raising flour
1 teaspoon ground cinnamon
1 teaspoon ground nutmeg
1 teaspoon ground allspice
½ cup apricot nectar

Spicy Nut Topping
¼ cup finely chopped walnuts
1 tablespoon sunflower kernels
½ teaspoon ground cinnamon
½ teaspoon ground nutmeg
½ teaspoon ground allspice

➤ PREHEAT OVEN to moderately slow 160°C.
1 Brush a deep, 20 cm square cake tin with melted butter or oil. Line base and sides with paper; grease paper. Using electric beaters, beat butter and sugar in small mixing bowl until light and creamy. Add the eggs gradually, beating thoroughly after each addition.
2 Transfer mixture to large mixing bowl; add fruit, walnuts and kernels. Using a metal spoon, fold in the sifted dry ingredients alternately with the apricot nectar. Stir until the mixture is almost smooth.
3 Spoon mixture evenly into prepared tin; smooth the surface.
To make the Spicy Nut Topping: Combine all the topping ingredients. Spoon mixture onto the top of the cake, pressing it down firmly with the back of the spoon.
Bake 2½ to 3 hours or until skewer comes out clean when inserted in centre of cake. Leave cake in the tin for 3 to 4 hours before turning out.

COOK'S FILE

Storage time: Because this cake does not contain alcohol, it should be eaten within 4 weeks of baking. Store in an airtight container.

1

3

BEST EVER RICH FRUIT CAKE

Preparation time: 45 minutes
Cooking time: 3 to 3 hours
    30 minutes
Makes one 20 cm round cake

250 g unsalted butter
1 cup soft dark brown sugar
5 eggs, lightly beaten
1 tablespoon coffee
    essence
1 teaspoon imitation vanilla
    essence
1 tablespoon molasses
1 tablespoon plum jam
¼ cup orange juice
2 teaspoons finely grated
    orange rind
1¼ cups/250 g sultanas
1¼ cups/250 g currants
1¼ cups/250 g raisins
⅔ cup/125 g chopped peel
½ cup/125 g glacé cherries, cut
    in halves
½ cup/100 g glacé apricots,
    chopped
½ cup/100 g glacé pineapple,
    chopped
½ cup/100 g figs, chopped
⅔ cup/80 g slivered almonds
2 cups plain flour
½ cup self-raising flour
2 teaspoons mixed spice
½ cup sherry, brandy or rum
¼ cup warmed, sieved
    apricot jam

Fondant Icing

1 kg pure icing sugar
5 teaspoons gelatine
¼ cup water
½ cup liquid glucose
1 tablespoon glycerine
1 cup pure icing sugar,
    extra, for kneading

Decorations

1 metre ribbon or lace
1 small posy of fresh flowers

➤ PREHEAT OVEN to slow 150°C.
Line base and side of a deep, 20 cm
round cake tin with greaseproof paper.
1 Using electric beaters, beat butter
and sugar in small mixing bowl until
light and creamy. Add eggs gradually,
beating thoroughly after each addition.
Add essences, molasses, plum jam,
juice and rind; beat until combined.
2 Transfer mixture to large mixing
bowl; add fruit and almonds. Using
metal spoon, fold in the sifted dry ingredients alternately with sherry. Stir
until just combined and the mixture is
almost smooth.
3 Spoon mixture evenly into prepared
tin; sprinkle top with cold water and
smooth surface with a wetted hand.
Tap cake tin gently on bench top to
settle mixture.
Wrap double thickness of brown paper
around tin, secure with paper clip.
Bake for 3 to 3½ hours or until skewer
comes out clean when inserted in
centre of cake. Leave cake in tin overnight before turning out.
4 To make Fondant Icing: Sift
icing sugar into large mixing bowl. In
small pan, dissolve gelatine in cold
water. Add glucose, place over gentle
heat, stirring occasionally until the
gelatine has dissolved. Remove from
heat, stir in glycerine. Cool 1 minute.
Make a well in centre of icing sugar
and pour in the gelatine mixture. Use
wooden spoon to thoroughly combine.
Knead by hand until mixture is a firm,
dough-like paste.
Turn mixture onto a smooth surface
lightly covered with sifted icing sugar.
Knead well until smooth and pliable;
mixture should resemble Plasticine.
Cover fondant securely with plastic
wrap until needed. Do not refrigerate.

Best used within 2 days of making.
5 To cover cake with fondant, place
cake upside down on a covered cake
board or large, flat plate. Brush cake
lightly and evenly with sieved jam.
Knead fondant with the extra sifted
icing sugar until smooth. Roll out
evenly on a smooth surface lightly
covered with icing sugar until 1 cm
thick; try to roll out in the shape of the
cake. Move icing constantly to prevent
it sticking to the work surface.
Lift onto cake using rolling pin. Roll

1

2

3

rolling pin gently onto top of cake. Ease the icing around sides and base of cake.

Coat the palms of your hands lightly with icing sugar and rub top and sides of cake lightly for 2 to 3 minutes until icing is smooth. Cut away excess from base using sharp knife.

Cake is best left for 2 days in a clean, cool place before decorating. Do not refrigerate.

6 Soften a small amount of icing to a paste with a little hot water. Wrap ribbon or lace around cake, secure with a little of the softened icing.

Hold in place with a pin until icing dries. Trim excess ribbon using small, sharp scissors. Tie a bow from remaining ribbon, place over ribbon join, using icing paste on back to secure. Place posy of small flowers on top of cake just prior to serving.

COOK'S FILE

Storage time: Uniced cake can be kept for up to 3 months. Store, covered in several layers of plastic wrap, in the refrigerator. Iced cake will keep for up to 3 months at room temperature. Keep in a cool, dark, dust-free place. Iced cake can also be frozen for up to 12 months. Store in freezer in a rigid plastic container.

Variation: Cake may be covered with 750 g purchased marzipan before adding fondant icing. Follow same instructions for fondant icing. Leave marzipan to dry for at least 24 hours before applying fondant.

4

5

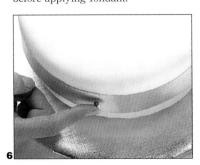

6

CLASSIC BOILED FRUIT CAKE

Preparation time: 30 minutes
Cooking time: 1 to 1 hour 15 minutes
Makes one 20 cm round cake

1¼ cups self-raising flour
1¼ cups plain flour
250 g unsalted butter
1 cup soft dark brown sugar
2 cups/375 g mixed dried fruit
1⅓ cups/200 g pitted prunes,
   chopped
1¼ cups port
½ teaspoon bicarbonate of soda
2 eggs, lightly beaten

➤ PREHEAT OVEN to moderate 180°C. Line the base and side of a deep, 20 cm round cake tin with greaseproof paper. Sift flours into large mixing bowl.
1 Combine butter, sugar, dried fruit, prunes and port in medium pan.
Stir over low heat until butter has melted and sugar has dissolved. Bring to the boil and simmer, uncovered, for 5 minutes.
2 Remove from heat, stir in soda and set aside to cool. Add eggs, mix well. Pour the mixture onto the sifted flours, mix well.
3 Pour mixture evenly into prepared tin; smooth the surface. Bake cake for 1 to 1¼ hours or until skewer comes out clean when inserted in centre of cake. Leave cake in tin 1 hour before turning out.

COOK'S FILE

Storage time: Store, covered with several layers of plastic wrap, for up to 2 months in the refrigerator.
Variation: Packeted mixed dried fruit was used; substitute any combination of your favourite dried fruits.

AMERICAN-STYLE FESTIVE FRUIT CAKE

Preparation time: 30 minutes
Cooking time: 1 to 1 hour 15 minutes
Makes two bar tin cakes

125 g unsalted butter
¼ cup soft brown sugar
2 eggs, lightly beaten
¼ cup golden syrup
250 g dates, pitted
125 g glacé pineapple, cut into
    2 cm pieces
125 g glacé apricots, cut into
    2 cm pieces
200 g whole red glacé cherries

125 g whole macadamia nuts
125 g whole brazil nuts
125 g whole hazelnuts
¼ cup self-raising flour
¼ cup plain flour
2 tablespoons port or brandy

▶ PREHEAT OVEN to slow 150°C. Line the bases and the sides of two 26 x 8 x 4.5 cm bar tins with greaseproof paper.

1 Using electric beaters, beat butter and sugar in small mixing bowl until light and creamy. Add eggs gradually, beating thoroughly after each addition. Add syrup; beat until combined.

2 Transfer mixture to large mixing bowl; add fruit and nuts. Using a metal spoon, fold in the sifted ingredients alternately with the liquid. Stir until just combined and mixture is almost smooth.

3 Spoon mixture evenly into prepared tins; smooth surface. Bake 1¼ hours or until skewer comes out clean when inserted in centre of cakes. Leave cakes in tins 1 hour before turning out.

COOK'S FILE

Storage time: Cake will keep in an airtight container in the refrigerator for up to 3 months.

Hint: Best served in thin slices. Cake can be baked in a ring tin, if desired. Decorate with Christmas ribbon and use as centrepiece for your table.

GREAT VALUE FRUIT CAKE

Preparation time: 1 hour
Cooking time: 3 to 3 hours 30 minutes
Makes one 20 cm square cake

250 g unsalted butter
1 cup soft brown sugar
4 eggs, lightly beaten
1 teaspoon imitation vanilla
  essence
1 tablespoons orange marmalade
1 tablespoon golden syrup
1.25 kg mixed dried fruit
2 cups plain flour
½ cup self-raising flour
2 teaspoons mixed spice
1 teaspoon ground cinnamon
½ cup rum, brandy or port

Royal Icing
4 egg whites
5½ cups pure sifted icing sugar
2 teaspoons lemon juice

Decorations
1 metre red, green or tartan
  ribbon
selection of small Christmas
  ornaments

➤ PREHEAT OVEN to slow 150°C. Line the base and the sides of a deep, 20 cm square cake tin with grease-proof paper.

1 Using electric beaters, beat butter and sugar in small mixing bowl until light and creamy. Add eggs gradually, beating thoroughly after each addition. Add essence, marmalade and golden syrup; beat until combined.

2 Transfer mixture to a large mixing bowl; add fruit. Using a metal spoon, fold in the sifted dry ingredients alternately with liquid. Stir until just combined and mixture is almost smooth.

Spoon mixture evenly into prepared tin; sprinkle top with cold water and smooth surface with wetted hand.

3 Tap cake tin gently on bench top to settle mixture. Wrap double thickness of brown paper around cake tin; secure with a paper clip. Bake cake for 3 to 3½ hours or until skewer comes out clean when inserted in centre. Leave cake overnight before turning out.

4 To make Royal Icing: Using electric beaters, beat egg whites in a clean, dry mixing bowl for 30 seconds. Add icing sugar, 1 tablespoon at a time, beating continuously on a slow speed until mixture is very stiff and stands in peaks. Blend in lemon juice. Cover with damp cloth or plastic wrap to prevent icing drying out.

5 Place cake on large plate or cake board. Using a flat-bladed knife, cover cake completely with icing, reserving 2 tablespoons for decoration. Use the knife to work icing into fluffy peaks all over the cake. Leave cake for 2 hours to allow icing to harden.

6 Wrap ribbon around cake, secure with small amount of Royal Icing. Trim excess ribbon, tie into a bow, trim edges. Place a small amount of Royal Icing on back of bow, place bow over ribbon join, secure with a pin; remove pin when icing is firm.
Position ornaments on cake, securing them with a small amount of icing.

C O O K ' S   F I L E

Storage time: Uniced cake can be kept for up to 3 months. Store, covered with several layers of plastic wrap, in the refrigerator. Iced cake will keep for up to 2 weeks at room temperature.
Hint: Royal Icing sets very quickly so it is important to work fast when icing the cake.
The icing may be coloured with food colourings from supermarkets or cake-decorating speciality shops.

1

2

3

4

5

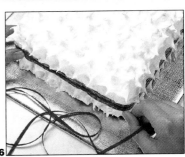

6

CURRANT CAKE

Preparation time: 25 minutes
Cooking time: 2 hours 30 minutes
  to 3 hours
Makes one 20 cm round cake

250 g unsalted butter
1 cup soft brown sugar
4 eggs, lightly beaten
2 tablespoons lime marmalade
1 kg currants
2 cups plain flour
1 teaspoon mixed spice
¾ cup whisky

➤ PREHEAT OVEN to moderately slow 160°C. Line base and side of a deep, 20 cm round cake tin with greaseproof paper.

1 Using electric beaters, beat butter and sugar in small mixing bowl until light and creamy. Add eggs gradually, beating thoroughly after each addition. Add marmalade; beat until combined.

2 Transfer mixture to large mixing bowl; add fruit. Using a metal spoon, fold in sifted ingredients alternately with whisky. Stir until just combined and mixture is almost smooth.

3 Spoon the mixture evenly into the prepared tin; smooth the surface. Bake for 2½ to 3 hours or until a skewer comes out clean when inserted in centre of cake. Leave cake in tin for several hours or overnight to cool.

COOK'S FILE

Storage time: Up to 2 months. Store, covered with several layers of plastic wrap, in the refrigerator.

Variation: Any flavour and texture of marmalade can be used.

Hint: The currants can be soaked overnight in half the measured amount of whisky (or brandy, if preferred). This will give a slightly moister cake.

BOILED GINGER FRUIT CAKE

Preparation time: 30 minutes
Cooking time: 1 to 1 hour 15 minutes
Makes one 20 cm square cake

1¼ cups self-raising flour
1¼ cups plain flour
250 g unsalted butter
1 cup soft dark brown sugar
1 cup/200 g dates, chopped
1 cup/200 g raisins
1 cup/200 g sultanas
½ cup/100 g chopped glacé
  ginger
⅔ cup green ginger wine
⅓ cup apple juice
2 teaspoons ground ginger
½ teaspoon bicarbonate of soda
2 eggs, lightly beaten

➤ PREHEAT OVEN to moderate 180°C. Line the base and the sides of a deep, 20 cm square cake tin with greaseproof paper.

1 Sift flours into large mixing bowl. Combine butter, sugar, fruits, ginger wine, juice and ground ginger in a medium pan. Stir over low heat until the butter has melted and the sugar has dissolved; bring to the boil and simmer, uncovered, for 5 minutes.

2 Remove from heat, stir in soda, set aside to cool. Add eggs and mix well. Add fruit mixture to flours, stir with a metal spoon until just combined; do not overbeat.

3 Pour mixture evenly into prepared tin; smooth surface.
Bake for 1 to 1¼ hours or until skewer comes out clean when inserted in centre of cake. Leave cake in the tin for 1 hour before turning out.

COOK'S FILE

Storage time: Up to 2 months. Store, covered with several layers of plastic wrap, in the refrigerator.

Variation: To add extra flavour and moistness, pour 2 tablespoons of green ginger wine over cake when it is still hot from the oven.

Opposite: Currant Cake (top),
Boiled Ginger Fruit Cake (bottom).

DUNDEE CAKE

Preparation time: 30 minutes
Cooking time: 2 to 2 hours
   30 minutes
Makes one 20 cm round cake

250 g unsalted butter
1 cup soft brown sugar
4 eggs, lightly beaten
1 cup/200 g raisins
1 cup/200 g sultanas
1⅓ cups/200 g currants
⅓ cup/60 g combined orange
   and lemon peel
¼ cup/60 g glacé cherries,
   chopped

1 cup/100 g almond meal
¾ cup/100 g slivered almonds
1½ cups plain flour
½ cup self-raising flour
2 tablespoons rum
100 g whole almonds, for
   decoration

➤ PREHEAT OVEN to slow 150°C.
1 Brush a deep, 20 cm round cake tin
with melted butter or oil. Line base
and side with greaseproof paper.
Using electric beaters, beat butter and
sugar in small mixing bowl until light
and creamy. Add the eggs gradually,
beating thoroughly after each addition.
2 Transfer mixture to large mixing
bowl; add fruits, peel and nuts. Using

a metal spoon, fold in the sifted dry
ingredients alternately with liquid. Stir
until just combined and the mixture is
almost smooth.
3 Spoon mixture evenly into the tin;
smooth surface. Arrange almonds on
top of cake. Bake for 2 to 2½ hours or
until skewer comes out clean when inserted in centre of cake. Leave cake in
tin several hours before turning out.

COOK'S FILE

Storage time: Up to 2 months. Store,
covered with several layers of plastic
wrap, in the refrigerator.
Hint: All traditional fruit cakes must
be left to cool in tin for the specified
time. If turned out hot, they will break.

LIGHT FRUIT CAKE

Preparation time: 35 minutes
Cooking time: 3 to 3 hours 30 minutes
Makes one 20 cm round cake

250 g unsalted butter
1 cup caster sugar
4 eggs, lightly beaten
1 teaspoon imitation vanilla
  essence
1 kg mixed dried fruit
1½ cups plain flour
½ cup self-raising flour
½ cup sherry
125 g assorted glacé fruits
60 g walnut halves

➤ PREHEAT OVEN to moderately slow 160°C. Line base and side of a deep, 20 cm round cake tin with greaseproof paper.

1 Using electric beaters, beat butter and sugar in small mixing bowl until light and creamy. Add eggs gradually, beating thoroughly after each addition. Add essence; beat until combined.

2 Transfer mixture to large mixing bowl; add dried fruit. Using a metal spoon, fold in sifted dry ingredients alternately with the sherry. Stir until just combined and mixture is almost smooth.

3 Spoon mixture evenly into prepared tin; smooth surface. Decorate top with glacé fruits and walnuts. Bake for 3 to 3½ hours or until skewer comes out clean when inserted in centre of cake. Leave cake in tin for several hours or overnight to cool.

COOK'S FILE

Storage time: Up to 1 month. Store, covered with several layers of plastic wrap, in the refrigerator.

Variation: Packeted mixed dried fruit has been used for this recipe but any combination of dried and glacé fruits to the same weight can be used. The alcohol and nuts used can also be varied, depending on your taste.

The glacé fruits and walnuts could be omitted for decoration and the cake iced, if preferred.

TWELFTH NIGHT CAKE

Preparation time: 45 minutes
Cooking time: 3 to 3 hours 30 minutes
Makes one 20 cm round cake

250 g unsalted butter
1 cup caster sugar
4 eggs, lightly beaten
2 teaspoons finely grated lemon
  rind
3½ cups/500 g currants
1 cup/155 g mixed peel
½ cup/60 g almonds, chopped
2 cups plain flour
½ cup self-raising flour
½ cup brandy
100 g glacé or crystallised
  orange and lemon slices, for
  decoration

Lemon Glaze
⅓ cup lemon juice
¼ cup icing sugar

➤ PREHEAT OVEN to moderately slow 160°C. Line the base and side of a deep, 20 cm round cake tin with greaseproof paper.

1 Using electric beaters, beat butter and sugar in small mixing bowl until light and creamy.
Add the eggs gradually, beating thoroughly after each addition. Add rind; beat until combined. Transfer the mixture to a large mixing bowl; add fruit and almonds.

2 Using a metal spoon, fold in sifted flours alternately with the brandy. Stir until just combined and the mixture is almost smooth. Spoon mixture evenly into prepared tin; smooth surface.

Bake cake for 3 to 3½ hours or until skewer comes out clean when inserted in centre of cake. Leave cake in tin for 20 minutes before turning onto wire rack. Do not remove lining paper.

3 To make the Lemon Glaze: Combine the lemon juice and sifted icing sugar, stir until well mixed. Pour the mixture over the warm cake. Leave to set for 5 minutes. Remove the lining paper and decorate the top of the cake with the orange and lemon slices.

COOK'S FILE

Storage time: Make up to 2 weeks ahead. Store, covered with plastic wrap, in the refrigerator.

Hint: Icing sugar is commercially made by milling granulated sugar to a fine powder. You can't achieve the same effect by using a food-processor.

WHISKY AND SPICE FRUIT CAKE

Preparation time: 45 minutes
Cooking time: 1 to 1 hour 15 minutes
Makes one 20 cm square cake

250 g unsalted butter
½ cup caster sugar
½ cup soft dark brown sugar
4 eggs, separated
3 cups/500 g raisins
1½ cups plain flour
1 cup self-raising flour
2 teaspoons mixed spice
1 teaspoon ground cinnamon
1 teaspoon ground cardamom
1 teaspoon ground cloves
¾ cup Scotch whisky

Honey Frosting
90 g cream cheese, softened
2 teaspoons honey
1 teaspoon finely grated lemon
   rind
1½ cups icing sugar

➤ PREHEAT OVEN to moderately slow 160°C. Brush a deep, 20 cm square cake tin with melted butter or oil. Line base and sides with paper; grease paper.

1 Using electric beaters, beat butter and sugars in small mixing bowl until light and creamy. Add the egg yolks gradually, beating thoroughly after each addition.

2 Transfer the mixture to a large mixing bowl; add the raisins. Using a metal spoon, fold in sifted dry ingredients alternately with whisky. Stir until just combined and the mixture is almost smooth.

3 Using electric beaters, beat egg whites in small mixing bowl until soft peaks form. Using a metal spoon, fold through cake mixture.

Spoon mixture evenly into prepared tin; smooth the surface. Bake for 1 to 1¼ hours or until skewer comes out clean when inserted in centre of cake. Leave cake in tin 20 minutes before turning onto wire rack to cool.

To make Honey Frosting: Beat cream cheese, honey and rind in small mixing bowl until light and creamy.

Add sifted icing sugar, beating for 3 to 4 minutes or until mixture is smooth and fluffy. Spread on top of cake.

COOK'S FILE

Storage time: Cake is best eaten within 1 week of making. Uniced cake can be kept for up to 3 weeks. Store in an airtight container.

1

2

3

CELEBRATION CAKES

PASSIONFRUIT TORTE

Preparation time: 15 minutes
Cooking time: 50 minutes
Makes one 23 cm round cake

200 g unsalted butter
1 cup caster sugar
3 eggs, lightly beaten
¼ cup fresh passionfruit pulp
2½ cups self-raising flour
⅔ cup milk
1¼ cups cream

Passionfruit Cream
½ cup caster sugar
¼ cup fresh passionfruit pulp
2 egg whites

➤ PREHEAT OVEN to moderate 180°C. Brush a deep, 23 cm round cake tin with melted butter or oil. Line base and side with paper; grease paper.
Using electric beaters, beat butter and sugar in a small mixing bowl until light and creamy. Add the eggs gradually, beating thoroughly after each addition. Add passionfruit pulp; beat until combined.
1 Transfer mixture to large mixing bowl. Using a metal spoon, fold in sifted flour alternately with milk. Stir until just combined and mixture is smooth.
Spoon mixture evenly into prepared tin; smooth surface. Bake 50 minutes or until skewer comes out clean when inserted in centre of cake. Leave cake in tin 15 minutes before turning onto wire rack to cool.
2 To make Passionfruit Cream: Combine sugar and passionfruit pulp in small pan. Stir constantly over low heat until mixture boils and sugar has dissolved. Simmer without stirring, uncovered, 3 minutes; remove from heat. Using electric beaters, beat egg whites in a clean, dry mixing bowl until stiff peaks form.
Pour hot passionfruit mixture in thin stream over egg whites, beating constantly until cream is thick, glossy and increased in volume.
3 Turn cake upside down. Cut horizontally into four layers. Divide the Passionfruit Cream into three even portions. Place first layer on a serving plate. Spread the cake evenly with the Passionfruit Cream.
Continue layering with remaining cake and Passionfruit Cream, ending with cake. Using electric beaters, beat cream in a small mixing bowl until stiff peaks form. Using a flat-bladed knife, spread the cream over top and side of cake.

COOK'S FILE

Storage time: This is best assembled and eaten the day it is made. It can be decorated up to 3 hours before serving. Store, uncovered, in the refrigerator.

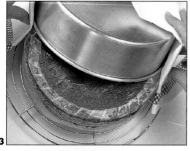

BLACK FOREST CAKE

Preparation time: 1 hour 15 minutes
Cooking time: 40 to 50 minutes
Makes one 23 cm round cake

200 g unsalted butter
¾ cup caster sugar
3 eggs, lightly beaten
1 teaspoon imitation vanilla
  essence
1⅔ cups self-raising flour
⅓ cup plain flour
¾ cup cocoa powder
1 tablespoon instant coffee
  powder
½ teaspoon bicarbonate
  of soda
½ cup buttermilk
⅓ cup milk
1¼ cups cream, whipped
425 g can pitted cherries,
  drained

white and dark chocolate curls,
  for decoration (see page 11)

Chocolate Mock Cream
200 g dark chocolate, chopped
250 g unsalted butter

➤ PREHEAT OVEN to moderate
180°C. Brush a deep, 23 cm round cake
tin with melted butter or oil, line base
and side with paper; grease paper.
1 Using electric beaters, beat butter
and sugar in small mixing bowl until
light and creamy. Add eggs gradually,
beating thoroughly after each addition.
Add essence; beat until combined.
2 Transfer mixture to large mixing
bowl. Using a metal spoon, fold in
sifted flours, cocoa, coffee and soda
alternately with combined buttermilk
and milk. Stir until just combined and
the mixture is almost smooth.
3 Pour mixture evenly into prepared
tin; smooth the surface. Bake for 40 to

50 minutes or until skewer comes out
clean when inserted in centre of cake.
Leave cake in tin 20 minutes before
turning onto wire rack to cool.
**4 To make Chocolate Mock
Cream:** Place chocolate in glass bowl.
Stir over barely simmering water until

melted; remove from heat. Beat butter in small mixing bowl until light and creamy. Add chocolate, beating 1 minute or until mixture is glossy and smooth.

5 Turn cake upside down. Cut into three layers horizontally. Place first layer on serving plate. Spread cake evenly with half the whipped cream, top with half the cherries. Continue layering with remaining cake, cream and cherries, ending with cake on top.

6 Spread Mock Cream over top and sides, using a flat-bladed knife. Using a piping bag, pipe stars of remaining mixture around cake rim. Decorate top with chocolate curls (refer to page 11).

(refer to page 11)

COOK'S FILE

Storage time: This cake and its filling is best assembled and eaten on the day that it is made.

ITALIAN LIQUEUR CAKE

Preparation time: 1 hour 30 minutes
Cooking time: 50 minutes
Makes one 20 cm round cake

1 cup self-raising flour
1 tablespoon cornflour
2 tablespoons rice flour
5 eggs, lightly beaten
¾ cup caster sugar
1 teaspoon imitation vanilla
   essence
80 g unsalted butter, melted
⅔ cup Marsala

½ cup orange marmalade
2 x 250 g punnets strawberries,
   one punnet sliced
2½ cups cream, whipped

Custard
¼ cup custard powder
¼ cup caster sugar
½ cup buttermilk
1 cup milk
1 teaspoon imitation vanilla
   essence
½ cup cream

➤ PREHEAT OVEN to moderate
180˚C. Brush a deep, 20 cm round cake

tin with melted butter or with oil.
1 Line base and side with paper;
grease paper. Dust the tin lightly with
flour, shake off excess. Sift dry ingredients three times onto greaseproof
paper. Using electric beaters, beat eggs
in large mixing bowl for 6 minutes or
until thick and pale.
2 Add sugar gradually, beating constantly until dissolved and mixture is
pale and glossy.
Using a metal spoon, fold in essence,
flours and butter quickly and lightly.
Spread mixture evenly into the
prepared tin. Bake for 50 minutes or
until the sponge is lightly golden and

shrinks from side of tin. Leave sponge in tin for 20 minutes before turning onto wire rack to cool.

3 To make Custard: Combine custard powder, sugar, buttermilk and milk in medium pan. Stir continuously over a low heat until mixture boils and thickens. Stir in essence and cream; remove from heat. Cool.

4 Cut cake horizontally into three layers. Brush each layer with Marsala and marmalade. Place first layer on serving plate. Spread cake evenly with half the custard, top with half the sliced strawberries. Continue layering with the remaining cake, custard and strawberries, ending with a cake layer. Spread three-quarters of the cream over the top and sides of the cake, using a flat-bladed knife. Using a piping bag, pipe stars of remaining cream around the rim. Decorate with whole strawberries.

COOK'S FILE

Storage time: This cake is best eaten the day after it is made. This will allow the liqueur to flavour the cake. Cover assembled, undecorated cake with plastic wrap. Store in refrigerator. Decorate the cake with whipped cream and whole strawberries 1 hour before it is served.

Hint: The custard will look curdled until it has boiled and thickened. It will then become smooth and glossy. Buttermilk has a rich, tangy flavour which is particularly appreciated in baked goods. Once, buttermilk was always drawn off butter and slightly soured during the churning. Today, to ensure consistency of product, it is obtained by treating skimmed or partially skimmed milk with a culture of lactic acid bacteria.

VANILLA RASPBERRY CELEBRATION CAKE

Preparation time: 45 minutes
Cooking time: 40 minutes
Makes one 23 cm round cake

150 g unsalted butter
¾ cup caster sugar
2 eggs, lightly beaten
2 teaspoons pure vanilla essence
1 tablespoon glucose syrup
1½ cups self-raising flour
½ cup buttermilk
100 g white chocolate, chopped
2 x 300 g packets frozen
   raspberries, drained, or
   2 punnets fresh raspberries

Vanilla Cream
2 cups cream
2 tablespoons icing sugar
½ teaspoon pure vanilla essence

➤ PREHEAT OVEN to moderate 180°C. Brush a deep, 23 cm round cake tin with melted butter or oil, line base and side with paper; grease paper.
Using electric beaters, beat butter and sugar in small mixing bowl until light and creamy.
1 Add the eggs gradually, beating thoroughly after each addition. Add the essence and glucose; beat until combined. Transfer mixture to large mixing bowl. Using a metal spoon, fold in sifted flour alternately with buttermilk. Stir until just combined and the mixture is almost smooth.
2 Pour mixture evenly into prepared tin; smooth surface. Bake 40 minutes or until skewer comes out clean when inserted in centre of cake. Leave cake in tin 15 minutes before turning onto wire rack to cool.
3 Place chocolate in glass bowl. Stir over barely simmering water until melted; remove from heat. Pour chocolate onto a marble or Laminex board in a 4-cm wide strip. Smooth surface. Allow chocolate to set.
Shave off strips with a vegetable peeler. Set aside. (If the weather is very warm, refrigeration may be necessary.)
To make Vanilla Cream: Place cream in small mixing bowl. Using electric beaters, beat until soft peaks form. Add sifted icing sugar and essence. Continue beating until firm peaks form.
4 Cut cake in half horizontally. Place first layer on serving plate. Top with raspberries; slightly squash onto cake with a fork. Sandwich with top cake layer. Spread Vanilla Cream over top and sides of cake using a flat-bladed knife. Smooth surface. Cover cake with white chocolate shavings (see page 11).

COOK'S FILE

Storage time: This cake is best assembled and eaten the day it is made.

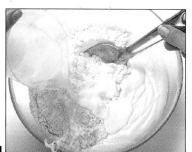

1

2

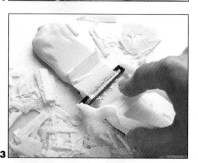

3

4

COFFEE HAZELNUT MERINGUE TORTE

Preparation time: 1 hour 15 minutes
+ overnight standing
Cooking time: 1 hour
Makes one 20 cm round layer cake

1½ cups/150 g roasted
   hazelnuts
4 egg whites
¾ cup caster sugar
⅓ cup plain flour
1¼ cups cream
1 tablespoon Tia Maria liqueur

Coffee Filling
½ cup caster sugar
2 tablespoons instant coffee
   powder
¼ cup water
4 egg yolks, lightly beaten
250 g unsalted butter, chopped

➤ PREHEAT OVEN to moderately slow 160˚C.
Brush bases of two 20 cm springform cake tins with melted butter or oil. Line the bases and sides with paper; grease paper.
Finely grind hazelnuts in an electric grinder or food processor. Set aside.
1 Place the egg whites in a small, clean, dry mixing bowl. Using electric beaters, beat until firm peaks form. Add the sugar gradually, beating constantly until dissolved and mixture is glossy and thick. Transfer mixture to

large mixing bowl; add nuts. Using a metal spoon, fold in sifted flour. Stir until just combined.
2 Divide meringue mixture into four even portions. Spread one portion over prepared base; smooth surface. Repeat with second portion. Bake 25 minutes or until lightly golden and crisp. Alternate trays halfway through cooking. Leave on trays 3 minutes; lift onto wire rack to cool. Repeat process with remaining meringue mixture.
3 **To make Coffee Filling:** Combine sugar, coffee powder and water in small pan. Stir constantly over low heat until the mixture boils and sugar dissolves. Simmer uncovered, without stirring, for 5 minutes. Remove from heat; cool for a further 5 minutes.
Using electric beaters, beat the egg yolks in small bowl on high speed for 10 minutes. With beaters still operating, pour warm syrup onto yolks, a few drops at a time. Continue to beat until all syrup is added and mixture is glossy and thick. Beat for 15 minutes or until the mixture has completely cooled. Add butter, a piece at a time, beating thoroughly after each addition. Place first meringue layer on a serving plate. Spread evenly with one-third of the filling. Continue layering with remaining meringue and filling, and ending with meringue on top.
4 Whip the cream in a small bowl until soft peaks form. Fold in liqueur. Cover the top and sides of the torte with the whipped cream mixture. Store in the refrigerator for several hours.

Remove from the refrigerator, leave for 10 minutes before serving.

COOK'S FILE

Storage time: Cake is best assembled and eaten on the day it is made.
Hint: Cake will cut better and be more moist if refrigerated for several hours before serving.
Always add the liqueur after cream has been whipped. If combined and whipped together, mixture may curdle.

SUPER-EASY APRICOT AND ALMOND GATEAU

Preparation time: 40 minutes
Cooking time: 40 minutes
Makes one 25 cm oblong cake

¾ cup self-raising flour
¼ cup plain flour
½ cup ground almonds
185 g unsalted butter
1 cup caster sugar
½ cup apricot nectar
3 eggs, lightly beaten
1 x 425 g can apricot halves,
　drained, juice reserved, sliced
2½ cups cream, whipped
½ cup flaked almonds,
　toasted

➤ PREHEAT OVEN to moderate 180°C. Brush a deep, 25 x 16 x 6 cm loaf tin with melted butter or oil, line base and sides with paper; grease the paper.

1 Sift flours into large mixing bowl. Add ground almonds. Make a well in the centre.
Combine butter, sugar and nectar in a medium pan. Stir over low heat until butter has melted and sugar has dissolved; remove from heat.

2 Add the butter mixture to the dry ingredients. Stir with whisk until just combined. Add eggs; mix well. Pour mixture into prepared tin; smooth the surface. Bake for 40 minutes or until skewer comes out clean when inserted in centre. Leave cake in tin 20 minutes before turning onto wire rack to cool.

3 Cut the cake into three layers horizontally. Brush each layer with the reserved apricot juice.
Sandwich layers together with cream. Using a flat-bladed knife, spread the cream over top and sides of cake.
Carefully press almonds around the sides of the cake. Decorate the top with apricot slices. Using a piping bag, pipe on cream swirls.

COOK'S FILE

Storage time: 2 days in the refrigerator without the toasted almonds. Sprinkle the almonds on just before serving.

Hint: Buy nuts as and when you need them; they quickly spoil and turn rancid, particularly in the heat. Store in an airtight container in a cool place.

1

2

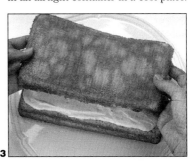

3

CHOCOLATE TRUFFLE CAKE

Preparation time: 2 hours
Cooking time: 30 to 35 minutes
Makes one 20 cm round layer cake

125 g cream cheese, softened
60 g unsalted butter
¾ cup caster sugar
2 eggs, lightly beaten
1 teaspoon imitation vanilla
   essence
¼ teaspoon red food colouring
60 g chocolate, melted
2 cups plain flour
¼ cup cocoa powder
1 teaspoon bicarbonate of soda
¾ cup water

Filling
250 g dark chocolate, chopped
⅓ cup cream
2 egg yolks

Icing
125 g dark chocolate, chopped
125 g unsalted butter

Truffles (makes 20; use 12)
150 g dark chocolate, chopped
50 g unsalted butter
2 tablespoons cream
¼ cup icing sugar
2 teaspoons rum or Grand
   Marnier
⅓ cup cocoa powder
¼ cup drinking chocolate

Chocolate Wedges
150 g dark chocolate, melted

➤ PREHEAT OVEN to moderate 180°C. Brush two deep, 20 cm round cake tins with melted butter or oil, line bases and sides with paper; grease the paper.

1 Using electric beaters, beat the cream cheese, butter and sugar in small mixing bowl until light and creamy. Add eggs gradually, beating thoroughly after each addition. Add essence, colouring and chocolate; beat until combined.
Transfer the mixture to a large mixing bowl. Using a metal spoon, fold in sifted flour, cocoa and soda alternately with water. Stir until just combined and the mixture is almost smooth.
Pour mixture evenly into prepared tins. Smooth surfaces; bake cakes for 30 to 35 minutes or until skewer comes out clean when inserted in centres of cakes. Leave cakes in tins 10 minutes before turning onto wire rack to cool.

2 To make Filling: Combine the chocolate and cream in a small pan. Stir over low heat until chocolate has melted; remove from heat. Whisk in egg yolks until mixture is smooth. Set aside.

3 To make Icing: Place the chocolate in a glass bowl. Stir over barely simmering water until melted; remove from heat. Beat the butter in a small mixing bowl until light and creamy. Add the chocolate, beating 1 minute or until the mixture is glossy and smooth. Set mixture aside.

4 To make Truffles: Combine the chocolate, butter, cream, sifted icing sugar and the liqueur in a small pan. Stir over low heat until chocolate and butter have melted; remove from heat. Transfer mixture to medium mixing bowl. Refrigerate for 15 minutes or until semi-set. Using electric beaters, beat the mixture until it is creamy.
Roll heaped teaspoonfuls of mixture into balls; roll in combined sifted cocoa and drinking chocolate to coat. Refrigerate until firm.

5 To make Chocolate Wedges: Cover the base of a 20 cm round cake tin with foil. Spread melted chocolate evenly over the foil, refrigerate until it is semi-set.

Using a sharp, flat-bladed knife, carefully mark chocolate into 12 wedges. Return to refrigerator until chocolate is completely set.

6 To assemble, cut the domes off both the cakes to give a level surface. Cut

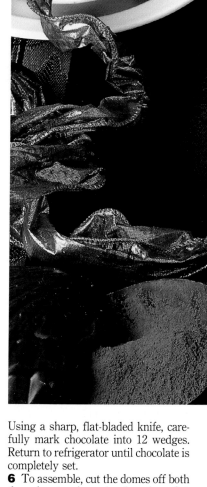

1

2

3

each cake in half horizontally. Place first cake layer on serving plate. Spread cake evenly with one third of the filling. Continue layering with the remaining cake and filling, ending with a cake layer on top.

Spread the icing evenly over top and side of cake using a flat-bladed knife. Decorate the top by placing 12 truffles around the rim of the cake. Position the chocolate wedges on cake, resting each one on a truffle.

COOK'S FILE

Storage time: Up to 4 days in the refrigerator.

Hint: Have cream cheese at room temperature to make it easier to work.

4

5

6

1

2

3

CHOCOLATE MOUSSE TORTE

Preparation time: 1 hour 30 minutes
+ 4 hours standing
Cooking time: 15 minutes
Makes one 20 cm square layer cake

4 eggs, separated
¼ cup icing sugar
½ cup self-raising flour
⅓ cup ground walnuts
200 g dark chocolate, chopped
2 tablespoons cocoa powder
1 tablespoon drinking chocolate
fresh berries, for decoration

Chocolate Mousse
100 g white chocolate, chopped
2 egg whites
2 tablespoons icing sugar
2 teaspoons gelatine
1 tablespoon hot water
1¼ cups cream, whipped
¾ cup grated milk chocolate

➤ PREHEAT OVEN to moderate 180°C. Brush two deep, 20 cm square cake tins with melted butter or oil, line bases and sides with paper; grease paper. Dust tins lightly with flour, shake off excess.

1 Place egg whites in small, clean, dry mixing bowl. Using electric beaters, beat until firm peaks form. Add the sifted icing sugar gradually, beating constantly until dissolved and mixture is glossy and thick. Add the beaten egg yolks; beat further 20 seconds. Transfer mixture to large mixing bowl.

2 Using a metal spoon, fold in sifted flour and walnuts quickly and lightly. Spread mixture evenly into prepared tins. Bake for 15 minutes or until the sponges are lightly golden and have shrunk from sides of tins. Leave in tins for 5 minutes before turning onto wire rack to cool.

3 To make Chocolate Mousse: Place chocolate in glass bowl. Stir over barely simmering water until melted; remove from heat. Place egg whites in small, clean, dry mixing bowl. Using electric beaters, beat until firm peaks form. Add sifted icing sugar gradually, beating constantly until dissolved. Combine gelatine with water in a small bowl. Stand bowl in hot water; stir until dissolved. Pour gelatine mixture in a thin stream over egg whites, beating constantly until well combined. Transfer mixture to large mixing bowl. Using a metal spoon, fold in chocolate, cream and grated chocolate.

4 Line a deep, 20 cm square tin with paper. Place one sponge in the base of tin. Pour mousse over the top; smooth surface. Place the second sponge on the top. Cover with plastic wrap, refrigerate for 4 hours or until set.

5 Melt chopped dark chocolate as for Step 3. Cover the base of a 32 x 28 cm oven tray with foil. Spread chocolate evenly over foil to cover the base of tray, swirl waves with the tines of a fork. Refrigerate until partially set. Carefully mark 6 cm squares with a sharp, clean, flat-bladed knife. You will need 20 squares for decoration. Return tray to the refrigerator until chocolate is completely set.

6 Lift cake from tin, using the lining paper to help. Carefully press the chocolate squares around the edges, overlapping each one. Sprinkle top of cake liberally with combined sifted cocoa and drinking chocolate. Decorate with fresh berries or seasonal fruits of your choice.

COOK'S FILE

Storage time: 1 day in the refrigerator.

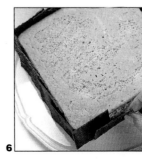

STRAWBERRY CHARLOTTE RUSSE

Preparation time: 1 hour
Cooking time: 20 minutes
+ 2 hours setting
Makes one 20 cm round cake

4 eggs, separated
¼ cup caster sugar
1 teaspoon imitation vanilla
   essence
½ cup self-raising flour
¼ cup plain flour
¼ cup desiccated coconut
110 g jar blackcurrant baby gel
2 x 125 g packets small sponge
   fingers

Strawberry Mousse
1 tablespoon gelatine
¼ cup orange juice
2 x 250 g punnets strawberries
⅓ cup caster sugar
1 tablespoon cream
2 eggs, separated
1¼ cups cream, whipped

➤ PREHEAT OVEN to moderate
180°C.
1 Brush a deep, 20 cm round
springform tin with melted butter or
oil, line base and side with paper;
grease paper. Dust tin lightly with
flour, shake off excess. Sift the flours

three times onto greaseproof paper.
Place egg whites in a small, clean, dry
mixing bowl. Using electric beaters, beat
until firm peaks form. Add sugar
gradually, beating constantly until dissolved and mixture is glossy and thick.
2 Add the beaten egg yolks; beat for
a further 20 seconds. Transfer mixture
to large mixing bowl.
Using a metal spoon, fold in essence,
flours and coconut quickly and lightly.
Spread mixture evenly into prepared
tin. Bake for 20 minutes or until the
sponge is lightly golden and has
shrunk from side of tin. Leave sponge
in tin 10 minutes before turning onto
wire rack to cool.
3 **To make Strawberry Mousse:**
Combine gelatine with orange juice in
small bowl. Stand bowl in hot water;
stir until mixture dissolves.
Place one punnet of strawberries, the
sugar, gelatine mixture, cream and egg
yolks in food-processor bowl. Using the
pulse action, press button for 20 seconds
or until mixture is smooth. Transfer
mixture to a large mixing bowl. Using
a metal spoon, fold in whipped cream.
Place egg whites in small, clean, dry
mixer bowl. Beat with electric beaters
until soft peaks form. Fold into strawberry mixture.
Reline springform tin with paper. Cut
dome off cake horizontally to give a
level surface. Place cake in lined tin.
Pour mousse evenly into prepared tin

to cover cake. Cover, refrigerate
several hours or until set.
4 Place the baby gel in a small pan.
Stir over a low heat until melted;
remove pan from the heat. Decorate
the top of the mousse with remaining

strawberries. Brush with baby gel until well coated. Remove cake from the tin. Place on a serving plate. Cut sponge fingers to the height of the cake. Press carefully around edges of cake. Secure with a ribbon if desired.

Storage time: Up to 3 days in the refrigerator without the addition of the sponge fingers; add the fingers just before serving.

Hint: For an attractive finish, baby gel makes an excellent, 'ready-made' glaze. You will find it is sold in small jars in the baby food section of your supermarket. It is also available in flavours other than blackcurrant.

SACHER TORTE

Preparation time: 40 minutes
Cooking time: 50 minutes
Makes one 20 cm round cake

1 cup plain flour
¼ cup cocoa powder
1 cup caster sugar
100 g unsalted butter
2 tablespoons strawberry jam
4 eggs, separated
2 tablespoons strawberry jam,
    extra, melted

Ganache Topping
150 g dark chocolate, chopped
¼ cup cream

➤ PREHEAT OVEN to moderate 180˚C. Brush a deep, 20 cm round cake tin with melted butter or oil, line the base and side with paper; grease the paper.
1 Sift the flour and cocoa into a large mixing bowl. Make a well in the centre. Combine sugar, butter and jam in small pan. Stir over low heat until the butter has melted and sugar has dissolved; remove from heat.
Add butter mixture to dry ingredients. Using a whisk, stir until just combined; add egg yolks, mix well.
2 Place egg whites in small, clean, dry mixing bowl. Using electric beaters, beat until soft peaks form. Using a metal spoon, fold egg whites into cake mixture.
Pour mixture into the prepared tin; smooth surface. Bake 50 minutes or until skewer comes out clean when inserted in centre of cake. Leave cake in tin 15 minutes before turning onto wire rack to cool.
3 To make Ganache Topping: Combine chocolate and cream in small pan. Stir over low heat until chocolate has melted and mixture is smooth. Remove from heat. Cool.
Cut the dome off the top of the cake horizontally. Turn the cake so that the base side is up. Brush cake with extra jam. Place on a wire rack set over a baking tray.

4 Pour Ganache Topping completely over cake. Smooth top and sides using a flat-bladed knife. Place remaining mixture in a piping bag and pipe the words 'Sacher Torte' across the top of the cake. Allow to set. Transfer cake carefully to serving plate.

COOK'S FILE

Storage time: 1 week in an airtight container or up to 3 months in the freezer uniced.

INDEX

CAKES

ICINGS, TOPPINGS AND FILLINGS

| | | | | | | | | | | | | | | | | | | | | | |
ruler markings (left margin): 1 cm, 2 cm, 3 cm, 4 cm, 5 cm, 6 cm, 7 cm, 8 cm, 9 cm, 10 cm, 11 cm, 12 cm, 13 cm, 14 cm, 15 cm, 16 cm, 17 cm, 18 cm, 19 cm, 20 cm, 21 cm, 22 cm

USEFUL INFORMATION

All our recipes are thoroughly tested in our test kitchen. Standard metric measuring cups and spoons approved by Standards Australia are used in the development of our recipes. All cup and spoon measurements are level. We have used eggs with an average weight of 60 g each in all recipes. Can sizes vary from manufacturer to manufacturer and between countries; use the can size closest to the one suggested in the recipe.

Australian Metric Cup and Spoon Measures

For dry ingredients the standard set of metric measuring cups consists of 1 cup, ½ cup, ⅓ cup and ¼ cup sizes.

For measuring liquids, a transparent, graduated measuring jug is available in either a 250 mL cup or a 1 litre jug.

The basic set of metric spoons, used to measure both dry and liquid ingredients, is made up of 1 tablespoon, 1 teaspoon, ½ teaspoon and ¼ teaspoon.

Note: Australian tablespoon equals 20 mL. British, US and NZ tablespoons equal 15 mL for use in liquid measuring. The teaspoon has a 5 mL capacity and is the same for Australian, British and American markets.

Ingredients in Grams (Aust. Cups)

	1 cup	1¼ cups	1½ cups	1¾ cups	2 cups
Breadcrumbs					
fine, fresh	60	75	90	105	120
dried	90	115	135	155	180
Cocoa Powder					
	85	105	125	150	170
Coconut					
desiccated	75	95	115	130	150
Flour					
	150	190	225	265	300
Sugar					
soft brown	165	205	245	285	330
caster	220	275	330	385	440
granulated	220	275	330	385	440
demerara	205	255	310	360	410
icing	160	200	240	280	320
raw	215	270	325	380	430

Oven Temperatures

Electric	C	F
Very Slow	120	250
Slow	150	300
Mod Slow	160	325
Moderate	180	350
Mod Hot	210	425
Hot	240	475
Very Hot	260	525

Gas	C	F
Very Slow	120	250
Slow	150	300
Mod Slow	160	325
Moderate	180	350
Mod Hot	190	375
Hot	200	400
Very Hot	230	450

British and American Cup and Spoon Conversion

Australian	British/American
1 tablespoon	3 teaspoons
2 tablespoons	¼ cup
¼ cup	⅓ cup
⅓ cup	½ cup
½ cup	⅔ cup
⅔ cup	¾ cup
¾ cup	1 cup
1 cup	1¼ cups

Glossary

Australian	British/American	Australian	British/American
Unsalted Butter	Unsalted Butter/Sweet Butter	Glacé Fruit	Glacé Fruit/Candied Fruit
125 g butter	125 g butter/1 stick of butter	Icing Sugar	Icing Sugar/Superfine Sugar
Bicarbonate of Soda	Bicarbonate of Soda/Baking Soda	Plain Flour	Plain Flour/All-Purpose
Caster Sugar	Castor Sugar/Superfine Sugar	Self-Raising	Self-Raising/Self-Rising
Cornflour	Cornflour/Cornstarch	Sultanas	Golden Raisins/Seedless White Raisins
Essence	Essence/Extract		

Manager Food Publications: Jo Anne Calabria
Home Economists – Recipe Origination: Kerrie Ray, Kerrie Carr, Voula Mantzouridis
Home Economists – Testing and Step-by-step Photography: Kerrie Ray, Tracy Rutherford, Melanie McDermott
Food Stylist: Carolyn Fienberg
Food Stylist's Assistant: Jo Forrest

Step-By-Step Photography: Reg Morrison
Photography: Jon Bader
Managing Editor: Lynn Humphries
Design and Art Direction: Lena Lowe

Publisher: Anne Wilson
Publishing Manager: Mark Newman
Production Manager: Catie Ziller
Marketing Manager: Mark Smith
National Sales Manager: Keith Watson

National Library of Australia Cataloguing-in-Publication-Data
Cakes: step-by-step.
Includes index
ISBN 0 86411 301 3
1. Cake.
641.8653

First printed 1993
Printed by Toppan Printing Co. Ltd, Singapore